Claudia Pereira da Silva
Rosângela Lopes Borges
Leidiane Dias de Paiva

Accessibility for students with disabilities in physical education classes

Claudia Pereira da Silva
Rosângela Lopes Borges
Leidiane Dias de Paiva

Accessibility for students with disabilities in physical education classes

Case study in municipal schools in the city of Caldas Novas/GO

Imprint

Any brand names and product names mentioned in this book are subject to trademark, brand or patent protection and are trademarks or registered trademarks of their respective holders. The use of brand names, product names, common names, trade names, product descriptions etc. even without a particular marking in this work is in no way to be construed to mean that such names may be regarded as unrestricted in respect of trademark and brand protection legislation and could thus be used by anyone.

Cover image: www.ingimage.com

This book is a translation from the original published under ISBN 978-613-9-72688-2.

Publisher:
Sciencia Scripts
is a trademark of
Dodo Books Indian Ocean Ltd. and OmniScriptum S.R.L publishing group

120 High Road, East Finchley, London, N2 9ED, United Kingdom
Str. Armeneasca 28/1, office 1, Chisinau MD-2012, Republic of Moldova, Europe
Printed at: see last page
ISBN: 978-620-7-89963-0

CLAUDIA PEREIRA DA SILVA

Undergraduate degree in Physical Education (UFG, 2003); Postgraduate degree in Physical Education (UFG, 2007); Specialisation in Teaching in Higher Education (APOGEU, 2010); Master's degree in Educational Sciences (Universidad Maria Serrana, 2017); PhD student in Educational Sciences (Universidad Del Sol).

claudinhaanjocaldas@hotmail.com

ROSÂNGELA LOPES BORGES

Graduated in Languages (Port./Ing.) (UEG, 2006); Postgraduate in Special Education (APOGEU, 2010); LIBRAS interpreter (ASG, 2011); Specialisation in Clinical and Institutional Psychopedagogy (UNINTER, 2017); Master's student in Professional and Technological Education (IFGoiano). She is currently a university lecturer and part of the Multidisciplinary Team of the Specialised Psychopedagogical Care Centre - NAPE, at the Caldas Novas College, in the state of Goiás, Brazil.

rosalb2@hotmail.com

LEIDIANE DIAS DE PAIVA

Degree in Pedagogy from the Faculty of Caldas Novas (UNICALDAS, 2018); Postgraduate student in Specialised Educational Assistance (AEE) (UNICESUMAR).

leidianepayva@hotmail.com

INDICE

INTRODUCTION

Physical activity has always been part of human daily life. Body movement has been around since Neanderthal man, even before writing. There are records of dances in the paintings and drawings found on cave walls. They used body movements to show their emotions and feelings, to communicate through rhythmic and repetitive gestures.

Throughout Brazilian history, physical exercise has undergone many changes. In the school sphere, there was the phase of physical exercise based on army techniques; the ban on women practising it; the introduction of gymnastics and later dance; making it compulsory in primary and secondary schools; making it a subject in all types of education; and the start of training for professionals to work in this area.

Currently, Physical Education is part of the Curriculum Matrix and is a compulsory subject in Primary Education, which covers from Kindergarten to High School. It was structured by the National Curriculum Parameters - PCNs (1997) into three blocks: 1) Sports, games, wrestling and gymnastics. 2) Rhythmic and expressive activities. 3) Knowledge about the body.

In addition to the concern for one's own body, hygiene and health, the PCNs (1997) are concerned with theoretical knowledge related to the physical structure of the human body, the rules of games and play; the historical context of the emergence of sports and dances; the affective, cognitive and socio-cultural dimensions of students.

It is understood that it is of the utmost importance to offer Physical Education as a subject in schools in order to promote the spread of good habits. Whether it's good nutrition, body posture, mastery and knowledge of their own bodies, body hygiene, physiological functioning or the importance of playing sport for a better quality of life, it is known that students are constantly influenced by their teachers. And this is one of the influences that can bring good results in the future and even a change in culture in relation to physical activities.

A sedentary lifestyle is one of the problems affecting humanity today. Everywhere in the world there are reports of overweight people, and this is also happening more and more among children. Practising physical activity accompanied by a good diet can help reduce the rate of diabetes, obesity and back problems among children. It also improves relationships and self-esteem.

Due to the compulsory inclusion of people with disabilities in mainstream education since 2008, schools have had to adapt their physical structure, curriculum and assessment methods to cater for this clientele. Special care has been taken in Physical Education classes, as scholars believe that this is the time to promote social inclusion and respect for others, regardless of colour, ethnicity, religion, gender or physical condition.

For this to happen, teachers with a degree in Physical Education need to be prepared to receive students with disabilities. It is hoped that, in addition to theoretical knowledge about the student's physical needs, the teacher will be able to integrate them into activities, games, plays and dances in the most "normal" way possible.

Given the importance of Physical Education for students' health and behaviour, the question arises as to how this subject has been applied to students with some kind of physical, motor or cognitive disability. The aim of this work is to find out how accessibility for this clientele occurs in this subject and to understand what pedagogical adaptations are being made by teachers in order to promote this integration.

To this end, this study is organised into five chapters:

Chapter I: Protocolary Framework, which outlines the objectives, the problem, the justification, the generic and secondary questions, as well as the delimitation of the topic.

Chapter II: Theoretical Framework, this chapter covers the history of Physical Education, the role of the teacher, the benefits of physical activities and the adaptations that need to be made to cater for students with disabilities.

Chapter III: Methodological Framework, which defines the type of research, the population and sample, the data collection techniques and instruments, and ethical considerations.

Chapter IV: Analytical Framework addresses the observations made and the analysis of the field research data, which will be transformed into graphs for a better visualisation and understanding of the results.

Chapter V: The aim of this chapter is to present the Final Considerations in relation to the bibliographical research and the field research, as well as to offer Recommendations for the problems identified.

CHAPTER 1

PROTOCOL MILESTONE

1.1 DESCRIPTION OF THE PROBLEM

Physical education at school is understood to be an element of the formal educational process, whose specific medium is physical activities carried out with an educational intent. It is recognised that it enables the development of the cognitive, affective-social and motor dimensions of children and adolescents through physical exercises, fights, games and dances.

According to the Federal Council of Physical Education - CONFEF (2002), Physical Education as a school subject "[...] introduces and integrates the student into the body culture of movement, forming the citizen who will produce it, reproduce it and transform it, enabling him [...] for the benefit of the critical exercise of citizenship and the improvement of the quality of life".

Inclusion, or the compulsory enrolment of students with disabilities in mainstream schools, has gone through several phases. Since the enactment of the first National Education Guidelines and Bases Law - LDBEN, Law No. 4.024/61, which guaranteed the right of "exceptional pupils" to education, establishing in its article 88 that in order to integrate them into the community these pupils should fit in, as far as possible, with the general education system.

Since then, various laws have been created and adapted until we reach the current reality of schools, where students are "obligatorily" included in regular education networks, but what we realise is that teachers are not prepared to work with this clientele, which requires, in a way, greater dedication and preparation on the part of the teacher.

Given the importance of this subject for students, education and society in general, the question arises as to how this subject has been applied to students with some kind of physical, motor or cognitive disability.

Physical Education, as a compulsory curricular component of basic education, cannot be indifferent to the inclusive education movement. As an integral part of the curriculum offered by schools, it is understood that this subject should contribute to school and social inclusion.

1.2 RESEARCH QUESTIONS

According to Lakatos and Marconi (2003), drawing up research questions saves time in the search process; keeps the focus on the need or problem; facilitates the critical evaluation of information as to its validity and applicability. The generic question is: How does accessibility occur for students with disabilities in Physical Education classes? Secondary questions: Are physical education teachers prepared to receive and work with students with disabilities?

Has physical education contributed to inclusion and interaction between all students? Do physical education classes show an understanding of limitations and abilities, stimulating the performance of students with disabilities?

1.3 RESEARCH OBJECTIVES

Research objectives are directly linked to a global and comprehensive view of the subject. They relate to "[...] the intrinsic content of both the phenomena and events and the ideas being studied". (PRODANOVI; FREITAS, 2013, p.124).

1.3.1 GENERAL AND SPECIFIC OBJECTIVES

To find out how accessibility occurs for students with disabilities in Physical Education classes.

To observe the importance of Physical Education and whether there is interaction with other students in the inclusion of students with disabilities; To investigate whether Physical Education classes show an understanding of limitations and capacities, stimulating the performance of students with disabilities; To analyse the pedagogical practices used by Physical Education teachers to work with students with disabilities.

1.4 BACKGROUND

Gadotti (1993) said that the search for an education for all that respects human rights, diversity and minorities is one of the great challenges facing Brazilian educators today. The aim is to eliminate stereotypes and replace the concept of equality with that of equity, i.e. equal rights while respecting differences.

Physical education classes, according to Bracht (1992), generally "[...] reinforce the apathy and discouragement of the less expressive, who are always discriminated against and often made to give up their place on the court, given their lack of mastery of sporting skills". This is because schools are preoccupied with highlighting those who already excel, rather than offering an activity that awakens in those "without physical skills" the desire to practise and improve.

Physical education and sports in general are of great importance to the development of individuals. When it comes to the care and development of people with disabilities, it is inferred that it should be aimed at: health, leisure, socialisation, inclusion, better performance in their daily activities, a better quality of life and consequently a "normal" life.

The aim of this study was to address the issue of accessibility for students with disabilities in Physical Education classes, with the aim of valuing the school and social inclusion of this clientele, according to their individualities and limitations, and based on the fact that education is a right for all.

This is due to the importance of democratising everyone's access to all possible activities, as guaranteed by the Brazilian Constitution itself, and the need for more public policies that not only serve, but fight for the rights of people with disabilities and ensure that they have a dignified life in every respect.

The instruments used in this study will be obtained in the municipality of Caldas Novas, Goiás, Brazil. Specifically in schools in the municipal education network that have students with disabilities enrolled. The intention is to carry out a survey of managers, teachers and parents of students with disabilities in order to understand how accessibility is being provided to this public in Physical Education classes.

In this context, there is free access to these educational institutions because the city, the town hall and the schools are where the author of this project works. It is understood that since she is a Physical Education teacher and is currently working in the Municipal Sports Department of the city in question, she will have easier access to the data that will be compiled and investigated.

CHAPTER 2

THEORETICAL FRAMEWORK

2.1 CONCEPTUAL FRAMEWORK

Physical Education: A set of planned and structured physical activities that studies and explores physical capacity and the application of human movement. The aim of physical education lessons is to improve students' physical fitness and health by carrying out physical exercises and body activities.

Teachers: Education professionals whose aim is to raise students' awareness of health, nutrition, the importance of physical activity and all its daily benefits.

Accessibility: Accessibility means the quality or character of what is accessible. Ease of approach, treatment or acquisition. Promoting equal opportunities for school pupils in all areas.

Performance: In general, physical performance results from a combination of all the physical and mental characteristics of the individual, in this case students with disabilities.

2.2 HISTORIC MILESTONE

It is well known that the role of schools since their inception has been to transmit culture from one generation to the next, respecting the level of development of each one and cherishing the well-being of the students. Therefore, as citizens, everyone has the right to education.

Therefore, when Physical Education is considered a compulsory curricular component, as of LDBEN No. 9.394/96, it is recognised that all students in Basic Education should take part in these classes regardless of colour, race, ethnicity or social class.

Physical education is a source of knowledge that is necessary for building a new citizen who is more complete, more integrated and more aware of his or her role in society. However, in order for this discipline to achieve its real objectives, it needs to be based on the guidelines of Brazilian education.

There is a range of authors who discuss inclusion, school accessibility for people with disabilities, the importance of Physical Education for the student, especially for the integration and insertion of this public into school activities, as well as society in general. This wealth of information can be seen in the following chapters.

2.2.1 HISTORY OF PHYSICAL EDUCATION

Since the dawn of civilisation, as soon as man stood on his own two feet, he has always needed the action of bodily movements. Primitive man's daily life was characterised above all by two major concerns: attacking and defending himself (RAMOS, 1982).

Oliveira (2006) explains that there is also physical activity among animals, but in humans it has developed more because they have perfected the technique of catching and throwing (opposing thumbs).

> The physical activities of prehistoric societies - within the natural, utilitarian, warrior, ritual and recreational aspects - were aimed at the struggle for life, rites and cults, warrior preparation, competitive actions and recreational practices (RAMOS, 1982, p. 17).

Dance, in particular, was used in prehistoric times, according to Oliveira (2006), as a form of play or as a ritual. It was used to show joy or sadness. Whether it was the success of a hunt, the birth of a child or the loss of a loved one, there was dancing.

The history of physical education includes those who study the past and present of human activities, seeking to understand their evolution. Castellani Filho (2008) explains that in prehistoric times there was a great concern with the development of brute strength, which was what the warriors wanted and not well-being.

The anatomical phase of physical education emerged in antiquity, among the Greeks, who aimed for bulging muscles, without exaggeration, from where slender athletes emerged, with a concern for morality. In Greece, on the other hand, physical education aimed to develop muscle mass without concern for morals or intellect. (CAPINUSSU, 2005).

In Eastern Antiquity, there were various contributions to physical activities such as swimming, rowing and martial arts. Ramos (1982) explains:

> [...] in Persia, India, China, Japan and other peoples, in contrast to the practice in the Western world, physical activities were, exceptionally, used more as a means of ritual or preparation for life (RAMOS, 1982, p.17).

In addition to these, the aforementioned author emphasises physical activities such as yoga, Cong Fou, Jiu-Jitsu, polo, boxing and stick fencing. Both were as accepted as the others among the Hindu, Chinese, Japanese and Persian peoples.

Plato (348 BC), a philosopher in Athens, referred to gymnastics as the union between body and thought. Oliveira (2006) explains physical activity in Athens and Sparta:

> In the universe of Western civilisation, it is necessary to highlight Greece, with the cities of Athens and Sparta, which referred to physical activity as an instrument of moral and spiritual formation, in other words, it has the great merit of not divorcing Physical Education from the intellectual and spiritual. (OLIVEIRA, 2006, p.21).

In Rome, there was great interest in the Greek Olympic games, but the aim was to use them for military training. This idea lasted until the Middle Ages, when knights had to be trained for the Holy War. The researcher Capinussú (2005) describes:

> [...] that knights should be trained for the Great Crusades and Holy Wars organised by the Church [...] What's more, in their leisure time, knights would play chess, backgammon and other table games popularised in Europe; they would go out on horseback hunting wild boar [...] they would play gymnastic games and run on foot. (CAPINUSSÚ, 2005, p. 54).

In times of peace, games and tournaments served to continually prepare knights or soldiers for a possible war. Ramos (1982, p.23) adds that perfected tin football and tennis, with the names "calcio" and "racket game" respectively, have their origins in the Middle Ages. In addition to these, two other disciplines that emerged during this period stand out: equestrianism and fencing.

In the 15th century, the Renaissance brought physical education aimed at the bourgeoisie and introduced physical exercises such as jumping, running, swimming, wrestling, pelota, dancing and fishing. This was because they used what they had at hand. The lower classes also held their own sports competitions and championships (CASTELLANI FILHO, 2008).

It wasn't until 1453, in Constantinople, that natural exercises gained strength and became a reinforcement in education. Ramos (1982) explains:

> [...] with the adoption of classical ideas, from the 18th century onwards in the West, interest in natural life manifested itself and exercises were used as agents of education, albeit in a theoretical and empirical way [...] (RAMOS, 1982, p.24).

According to the same author, physical exercise took on a highly significant role, and this favoured the emergence of the discipline of Physical Education. Names such as Erasmus of Rotterdam (1466-1536), John Calvin (1509-1564), Jean-Jacques Rousseau (1712-1778) and Johann Heinrich Pestalozzi (1776-1827), among other great names, brought their contributions, both theoretical and practical, which greatly influenced the educational action that led to the great movement to systematise gymnastics.

The Modern Age saw the systematisation of gymnastics, favouring the emergence of the gymnastic movements of the Centre, in Germany, where "apparatus such as the fixed bar and the parallel bars were created, and the Germans were therefore the forerunners of the sport that today is called Olympic gymnastics" (OLIVEIRA, 2006, p.41). The practice of sports games in England and the emergence of the first studies into psychomotricity.

For cultural, political and professional reasons, physical activity has not always been part of the educational framework. It is understood that the emergence of localised gymnastics equipment brought greater muscular power and numerous sports preparation systems. Nowadays, this activity is associated with the figure of a healthy person. It is also used as therapeutic rehabilitation.

2.2.1.1 *PHYSICAL EDUCATION AS A DISCIPLINE*

Physical education as a school subject enables the development of the cognitive, affective-social and motor dimensions of children and adolescents through gymnastic exercises such as games, sports, dances and fights (BRACHT, 1992).

It wasn't until the 18th century, the Renaissance period, that gymnastics was received with greater emphasis in schools. At the La Giocosa school in Mantova, Italy, in 1423, Vittorino da Feltre (1378-1446) was established as the first educator to place the education of the body on the same level as the disciplines considered intellectual (MARINHO, 1980).

The aforementioned author adds that in 1762, Jean Jacques Rousseau (17121778) published the work "Emilio ou de la Educación" in which the importance of exercising the body and the spirit was emphasised. Physical education played an important role in the concept of education. 12 years later, Johann Bernard Basedow (1723-1790), in Germany, established his model school "Philanthropinum" where gymnastics was included in the school curriculum and had the same status as intellectual subjects.

Christian Gotthilf Salzmann (1744-1811), born in 1784, was a German pedagogue who emphasised the importance of sensory education for physical training and the development and improvement of students' intellectual capacity. In 1785, women were included in physical activities that were predominantly for men. Johann Christoph Guts Muths (1759-1839), also a German educator, founded the first women's gymnastics school where physical exercises were adapted to the sex (CASTELLANI FILHO, 2008).

The same author says that in 1794, Gerhard Ulrich Anton Vieth (1763-1836) published his work "Essays on an Encyclopaedia of Bodily Exercises" in which he discussed the importance of physical exercise for the moral and physical formation of the individual and persisted in making physical education compulsory in schools and universities.

Faria Júnior and Farinatti (1992) say that Vivat Victorius Franziskus Nachtegall (17771847), a Danish educator, inaugurated his private outdoor gymnasium in 1799. He was the first to suggest the use of mattresses as a form of protection.

In the 19th century, there was a great development in public education for the masses. Denmark, therefore, became the first country to require the teaching of Physical Education in public primary and secondary schools, administered daily outside of school hours. (FARIA JÚNIOR; FARINATTI, 1992).

Marinho (1980) explains that Johann Heinrich Pestalozzi (1746-1827) founded his educational institute in 1804, where he argued that "[...] movement was a natural need, indispensable to the child, and Physical Education, a means of sensory and aesthetic development, essential in education and health." Friedrich Frobel (1782-1852), a German pedagogue, founded the kindergarten (now Early Childhood Education) 20 years later, emphasising the importance of maintaining a vigorous and active body.

In 1864, Ellin Falk (1872-1942), Inspector of Gymnastics at Stockholm Elementary Schools, created modern gymnastics for children, adapted to the child's psychic characteristics and playful needs. At the same time, Germany was experiencing new objectives for physical activity in schools, emphasising the values of honesty, fair play, sportsmanship, individual effort, initiative and courage (MARINHO, 1980).

Castellani Filho (2008) comments that the American Association for the Advancement of Physical Education (AAAPE) was founded in 1892. John Dewey (1859-1952) contributed greatly, as he recommended changes to the educational process, with a focus on the child. He proposed an environment in which children could experience social and psychomotor experiences.

In 1945, Maurice Baquet (1911-2005) founded the French National Sports Institute (INS) and introduced sport into primary and secondary schools. The aim was, through games and sports competitions, "[...] initiation to progressive effort, dosed in relation to the age and physiological possibilities of the children and technical initiation to any sport". (CASTELLANI FILHO, 2008, p.56).

In the 1960s, psychomotricity was introduced into children's physical education with a re-educational and therapeutic focus. In addition to gymnastics and sport, it incorporated dance, games and play (FARIA JÚNIOR: FARINATTI, 1992).

In 1999, a worldwide survey carried out in Berlin (in both rich and poor countries) detected a decline in school physical education due to the inability of schools to adequately teach physical activities. The possibility of abolishing this subject was then debated (CASTELLANI FILHO, 2008).

The author goes on to explain that in Brazil in the 19th century, Physical Education was more associated with military institutions and the middle classes. It had a hygienist objective, which aimed to improve the health of the population. Due to the large number of slaves at the time, Physical Education worked alongside sex education, sensitising Brazilians to maintain the "purity" and "quality" of the white race.

It wasn't until 1837 that gymnastics, swimming, horse riding and dance were introduced in the municipality of Rio de Janeiro (then the country's capital). Gymnastics was included in the school curriculum in 1854, and dance in 1855. In 1885, gymnastics became compulsory in the school curriculum (CASTELLANI FILHO, 2008).

2.2.2 THE BENEFITS OF PHYSICAL EDUCATION

For João Freire, bodily movement should be interpreted as a valuable pedagogical resource in primary school, especially in the first segment of education, because "[...] the hand writes what the mind thinks about the world with which the child interacts." (FREIRE, 1992, p. 25). (FREIRE, 1992, p. 81).

Vygotsky explains that when playing, the child interprets the actions of adults, for him "[...] the child's play is not a simple recollection of what has been experienced, but the creative transformation of impressions into the formation of a new reality." (VYGOTSKY, 1998, p. 12).

Kichimoto (1993) states that:

> [...] Through play, children learn to co-operate with their playmates [...]. To obey the rules of the game [...], to respect the rights of others [...], to accept authority [...] to take responsibility, to accept penalties imposed on them [...], to give opportunities to others [...], to live in society. (KICHIMOTO, 1993, p. 110).

According to Portal Educação (2014), the aim of Physical Education is to spread knowledge about the human body, to improve and rehabilitate bodily health. Regarding sports, it shows their rules, modalities and behaviours.

To this end, Physical Education should teach theoretical knowledge such as the history of the emergence of sports, their rules and fundamentals. As well as practical functional principles and body positioning (CONFEF, 2002).

Ferreira (2011) argues that physical education is a very important subject because it improves the health of students from a very young age. It has many benefits, but it is very important to include this subject in all schools and for all ages.

According to the aforementioned author, when physical activity is included regularly in schools, it helps to avoid a sedentary lifestyle and obesity, strengthens muscles and improves cardiovascular health, improves the absorption of nutrients, aids the digestive process and increases metabolism. It also improves motor coordination and relieves stress.

> [...] it is understood that Physical Education is an area of knowledge of the body culture of movement and school Physical Education is a subject that introduces and integrates the student into the body culture of movement, forming the citizen who will produce it, reproduce it and transform it, equipping them to make use of games, sports, dances, fights and gymnastics for the benefit of the critical exercise of citizenship and the improvement of quality of life. (RODRIGUES, 2013, p. 01).

The author explains that play at school is of the utmost importance and differs from play at home in that it is worked on with objectives and not play for play's sake. Physical activity in schools has a positive influence on the student's personality, character and self-esteem. It increases their ability to concentrate and communicate, as well as helping them to get along as a team and respect others. According to Ferreira (2011), students learn to deal with each other's limitations, respecting ethnic, social, physical and moral differences.

The production of endorphins, the hormone responsible for giving pleasure to the practitioner, is released during physical exercise. It can be inferred that the main objective of Physical Education is to bring about not only physical health, but also psychological health. It is "[...] capable of achieving and provoking in the student a feeling of freedom and lightness of thought never experienced before, because it is engaged in developing and improving the body and mind.". (MIQUELIN; FERNANDES et al, 2014, p. 14).

2.2.3 ADAPTED PHYSICAL EDUCATION

Since the Federal Constitution (1988), which states in Article 5° that "Everyone is equal before the law, without distinction of any kind" and later the Law of Guidelines and Bases of National Education, No. 9.394/96, in its Article 58, which describes Special Education as "[...] the modality of school education, offered preferably in the regular school network, for students with special needs." it is increasingly common to find students with disabilities in schools.

According to Sassaki (1997) apud Cidade and Freitas (2002) inclusion is:

> [...] a process that requires transformations, small and large, in the physical environments and the mentality of all people, including the person with special needs themselves, with the aim of achieving a society that not only accepts but also values individual human differences, through understanding and co-operation. (SASSAKI, 1997, apud CIDADE; FREITAS, 2002, p. 26).

Mantoan (2003, p.17) defines inclusion as "[...] changing society, adapting it to receive people with disabilities". For the author, it's not enough for students to adapt in order to be included in school, it's necessary for the school to change in order to receive the students. Inclusion is therefore expected to bring about a change in the educational perspective.

It is known that even in the face of the guarantee in Brazilian law, schools are still not prepared to receive students with disabilities. According to Brito and Lima (2012, p.05), this can be seen in the "[...] lack of preparation on the part of teachers, who don't feel qualified to carry out the work of inclusion". It is also worth noting that students with disabilities are often made fun of by their classmates.

Adapted Physical Education is one of the areas of knowledge within Physical Education that aims to include people with disabilities in activities such as games, sports and exercise. It arose from the fact that these students are often excluded from classes because of their condition.

Cidade and Freitas (2002) define Adapted Physical Education as:

> Adapted Physical Education is an area of physical education whose object of study is human motor skills for people with special educational needs, adapting teaching methodologies to meet the characteristics of each disabled student, respecting their individual differences. (CIDADE; FREITAS, 2002, p. 27).

Gorgatti and Costa (2005) add that Adapted Physical Education is an emerging field of physical education, where the teacher must be patient, observant and creative. According to the authors, it emerged in 1950, defined by the American Association as diversified activities for people with disabilities who were unable to follow the rigorous programmes of the time.

There is no perfect standard or model for adaptation. Adapted Physical Education does not differ from regular Physical Education in its content, but comprises techniques, methods and forms of organisation that can be applied to students with disabilities (SILVA; SEABRA JÚNIOR; ARAÚJO, 2008).

The big challenge, according to the aforementioned authors, lies in the role and attitude of the PE teacher. Teachers need to be creative and capable of adapting lessons according to the disabilities that arise. This requires planning that combines procedures to break down barriers to learning and meet the needs of their students.

According to Cidade and Freitas (2002, p. 27) "Adapted Physical Education officially appeared in undergraduate courses through Resolution 03 of the Federal Council of Education, of 16 June 1987, providing for the work of Physical Education teachers with people with disabilities and other special needs". This document envisaged full curricula capable of offering Physical Education undergraduates a General, Humanistic, Technical and even Philosophical education.

2.2.4 The PHYSICAL EDUCATION TEACHER

In the United States in 1857, it was proposed that all teachers hired should learn a system of gymnastics adapted to all primary school grades. This was the first time in history that specific training was required for these professionals (FARIA JÚNIOR; FARINATTI, 1992).

According to the authors cited above, the North American Gymnastics Union Normal School opened in 1866. Lasting one year, in the evening, students studied: the history and aims of Physical Education; anatomy; first aid; dance and gymnastics combined with teaching methods.

Physical education curricula in the 19th century emphasised the practice of formal exercises. It was taught in regular classrooms, bringing together a large number of students in a small space, and teachers were not pedagogically prepared to teach physical activities (FERREIRA, 2011).

According to Ferreira (2011), despite intentions to implement Physical Education in schools, there was a lack of teachers who could administer it competently. It was only in 1929 that the Provisional Physical Education Course was created at the Infantry Sergeants' School, which graduated 22 public elementary school teachers.

It can be seen that Physical Education is an extremely important subject in the school curriculum, because it makes a significant contribution to the teaching-learning process, making teaching more dynamic. Therefore, it is up to the teacher to encourage their students to always take part in activities, always emphasising that this practice will help them, improving their quality and making them aware of their abilities and capacities to perceive and interact with their surroundings. In addition, for the author, it is the most loved subject in the school curriculum because it takes place in a playful way (RODRIGUES, 2013).

It is believed that all scientific and technological transformations will be accompanied by changes in cultural and ethical standards. In this way, the training of Physical Education professionals cannot be achieved to a merely practical-theoretical or intellectual extent, considering the current demands of our society and the labour market (BRITO; LIMA, 2012).

For the aforementioned authors, the basic requirements of a professional education for the Physical Education teacher should include being aware of their responsibilities as a teacher, to disseminate and implement theoretical and practical knowledge about human motricity; to optimise their potential to move in a specific or generic, harmonious and effective way; to train themselves to adapt, interact and transform society, always in search of a better quality of life; to demonstrate interest, enthusiasm, vibrancy, motivation and/or satisfaction with teaching.

2.3 LEGAL MARK

Several laws have emerged in Brazil seeking to make physical activity more effective. One of the first was in 1854, the Regulation of Primary and Secondary Instruction of the Municipality of Corte, which included gymnastics in the basic education of public schools. In 1855, the regulations for the Colégio D. Pedro II were approved, which provided for the teaching of dance and gymnastic exercises during recess. In 1876, another regulation at the same school left it up to the deans whether or not to exempt students from these activities. The others would receive a mark for their discipline (RAMOS, 1982).

An opinion was issued in September 1882, which provided for gymnastics for boys and calisthenics (a kind of rhythmic gymnastics, without the use of apparatus) for girls. Approved on 6 November 1883, the internal regulations for public primary schools provided for the practice of exercises during the breaks between classes, of half an hour each (MARINHO, 1980).

Imperial Decision No. 71 of 23 November 1885 made gymnastics compulsory in the primary school curriculum. Granted by Getúlio Vargas on 10 November 1937, Physical Education became compulsory in all primary and secondary schools, as well as in teaching courses. The 1937 Constitution was the first mention of Physical Education in federal constitutional texts. It included physical education as a compulsory educational practice, but not as a curricular subject (FARIA JÚNIOR; FARINATTI, 1992).

From 1939 onwards, there was a preoccupation with the professional training of Physical Education teachers. Schools of Physical Education were created in the states of São Paulo and Espírito Santo. Decree No. 1.212, of 17 April 1939, created the National School of Physical Education and Sports - ESEF, at the University of Brazil, now the Federal University of Rio de Janeiro - UFRJ (CASTELLANI FILHO, 2008).

When the first National Education Guidelines and Bases Law - LDB No. 4.024/61 - was passed, there was no mention of Physical Education at all. For this reason, a preliminary draft of this law was created, No. 4024/61, which made Physical Education compulsory in primary and secondary schools, up to the age of 18. Later, in the second LDB No. 5.692/71, the compulsory nature of school physical education at all levels of primary and secondary education was made quite explicit (OLIVEIRA, 2006).

2.3.1 1996 GUIDELINES AND BASES LAW

The same author goes on to point out that even though Physical Education was made compulsory, it was only with the enactment of the National Physical Education Policy Law No. 6.251/75 that sports practice was given a more explicit direction. Then, the third LDB 9.394/96 began to refer to Physical Education as a curricular component integrated into the school's pedagogical proposal.

The LDB (1996) describes the curriculum and compulsory nature of Physical Education as follows:

> Art. 26: Primary and secondary education curricula must have a common national basis, to be complemented, in each education system and school, by a diversified part, required by the regional and local characteristics of society, culture, economy and clientele.
> [...]
> § 3 Physical education, integrated into the school's pedagogical proposal, is a compulsory curricular component of basic education, and its practice is optional for students:
> I - who works six hours or more;
> II - over thirty years of age;
> III - who is performing initial military service or who, in a similar situation, is obliged to practise physical education;
> IV - protected by Decree-Law No. 1,044 of 21 October 1969;
> V - (VETOED)
> VI - who has offspring.

It should be noted that even though it was a compulsory component, even in 1996 it was optional for students to attend these classes as long as they met one of the requirements listed above.

2.3.2 NATIONAL CURRICULUM PARAMETERS **of 1997**

In order for it to become a curricular component, it was necessary to create a parameter for its application, just like the other disciplines. This led to the creation of the National Curriculum Parameters - PCNs (1997), which point to Physical Education as "[...] important, as it enables students to develop body skills, provide leisure time, the possibility of expressing feelings, affections and emotions." (brasil, 1997). (BRASIL, 1997).

The PCNs, mentioned above, have humanisation as one of their objectives:

> The Physical Education document puts forward a proposal that seeks to democratise, humanise and diversify the pedagogical practice of the area, seeking to broaden it from a purely biological vision to work that incorporates the students' affective, cognitive and socio-cultural dimensions. It incorporates, in an organised way, the main issues that teachers should consider when developing their work, supporting discussions, planning and evaluations of the practice of Physical Education in schools. (BRASIL, 1997, p.10).

This document also includes the aim of enabling students to have the opportunity to develop body skills from an early age and to take part in cultural activities such as games, sports, wrestling, gymnastics and dance, for leisure purposes and to express feelings, affections and emotions (BRASIL, 1997).

Nowadays, therefore, Physical Education can no longer be seen as a simple practice of physical exercises, skills or abilities, but is intended to "[...] enable the individual to reflect on their bodily possibilities and, with autonomy, exercise them in a socially and culturally significant and appropriate way". (BRASIL, 1997, p.22).

With regard to people with disabilities, the Physical Education Curriculum Parameters (1997) advocate their participation in activities. The document emphasises that "Participation in this class can bring many benefits to these children, particularly with regard to the development of affective capacities, integration and social insertion.". (BRASIL, 1997, p. 26).

There are some safety guarantees that the PE teacher should take into account, such as getting to know the disability they are going to work with, talking to parents about body movements and adverse behaviour and in some cases even having medical supervision or authorisation to carry out physical activities. (BRITO, 2012).

Subsequently, the teacher must "[...] make adaptations, create situations in order to enable the participation of special pupils." (BRASIL, 1997, p. 31). (BRASIL, 1997, p. 31). According to the document, a wheelchair user can be pushed in a race, and a student with limited mobility can stand in the goal in a football match, for example.

> The Physical Education class can favour the construction of a dignified attitude and self-respect on the part of the disabled person, and living with them can make it possible to build attitudes of solidarity, respect and acceptance, without prejudice. (BRASIL, 1997, p. 31).

According to the PCNs (1997), Physical Education content is chosen according to the criteria of: Social Relevance, Characteristics of the students and Characteristics of the area itself. They are organised into three blocks: Sports, games, fights and gymnastics; Rhythmic and expressive activities; Knowledge about the body. Both can be worked on together or separately, because they intersect and articulate with each other.

In the Body Knowledge block (BRASIL, 1997, p.36), students should study:
1. Knowledge of anatomy refers mainly to muscle and bone structure and is approached from

the point of view of the perception of one's own body [...].
2. Knowledge of physiology is basic to understanding the changes that occur during physical activity [...].
3. Knowledge of biomechanics is related to anatomy and mainly involves adjusting postural habits, such as lifting a weight and balancing objects [...].
4. Biochemistry will cover content that subsidises physiology: some metabolic processes of energy production, elimination and replacement of basic nutrients [■■■]■
5. Motor skills should be learnt throughout school, from a practical point of view, and should always be contextualised in the content of the other blocks.

With regard to the Sports, Games, Fights and Gymnastics block (BRASIL, 1997, p.38), it should be offered to Physical Education students:
1. pre-sports games: burnout, pique-bandeira, ball wars, pre-sports football games (goal-to-goal, control, kick-on-goal-rebatidadrible, bobinho, two-touch);
2. popular games: bocce, knitting, batting, bowling;
3. games: hopscotch, jump rope, elastic, hula hoop, marbles, spinning tops, kites, handkerchiefs, run-and-gun, hide-and-seek, catch-and-release, rabbits-in-the-trenches, hard-or-soft, squat, mother-of-the-street, go-carts, tug-of-war, etc;
4. athletics: speed, endurance, hurdles and relay races; long jump, high jump, triple jump and pole vault; weight throw, hammer throw, javelin throw and discus throw;
5. team sports: football, futsal, basketball, volleyball, beach volleyball, handball, futsal, etc..;
6. sports with sticks and rackets: baseball, table tennis, field tennis, ping pong;
7. sports on wheels: hockey, in-line hockey, cycling;
8. fights: judo, capoeira, karate;
9. gymnastics: health maintenance (aerobics and bodybuilding); preparation and improvement for dance; preparation and improvement for sports, games and fights; Olympic and rhythmic sports.

This block also includes historical information on the origins and characteristics of sports, games, wrestling and gymnastics, as well as an appreciation of these practices. It can be adapted, contracted or extended according to the region and location.

Rhythmic and Expressive Activities, which is the third block, deals with manifestations of body culture whose common characteristics are the "[...] intention of expression and communication through gestures and the presence of sound stimuli as a reference for body movement.". (BRASIL, 1997, p. 38). In simpler terms, these are dances and singing games.

These are suggestions from that block:
1. Brazilian dances: samba, baião, waltz, quadrilha, afoxé, catira, bumbameu-boi, maracatu, xaxado, etc..;
2. urban dances: rap, funk, break, pagode, ballroom dancing;
3. classical, modern, contemporary and jazz dances;
4. dances and choreographies associated with musical events: blocos de afoxé, olodum, timbalada, trios elétricos, samba schools;
5. nursery rhymes;
6. circle games, cirandas;
7. slaves.

With regard to student assessment of the contents of the three blocks, the PCNs (1997) emphasise that it is not a question of "physical strength tests" or standardised assessment that expects the same result from everyone. It should provide an opportunity for students to recognise themselves and for teachers to set new goals to improve their performance.

The National Education Council, in its Resolution of 18 February 2002, Cne/Cp 1, establishes National Curriculum Guidelines for the Training of Basic Education Teachers, at higher education level, full degree course. And according to the Regional Council of Physical Education of the 14th Region of Goiás and Tocantins - CREF, these guidelines make no reservations about the working environment of these professionals.

That's why, in 2013, the Federal Regional Court of the First Region, in Civil Appeal No. 0013853-04.2011.4.01.3500/GO, ruled that physical education graduates should not be allowed to work in clubs, gyms, parks or any non-school environment.

Bachelor's and Licentiate's degrees in Physical Education have their own specific legislation, have their own purpose and integrality, different workloads and subjects, different areas of knowledge and different professional interventions. For this reason, the National Education Council Chamber of Higher Education establishes that the Bachelor's Degree in Physical Education cannot work in educational environments, because "The Basic Education Teacher, with a full degree in Physical Education, must be qualified to teach this curricular component in basic education". (BRASIL, 2004, Art. 3).

The Federal Regional Court of the First Region (2013), cited above, also establishes that there must be a complementary "dual qualification" in Bachelor's or Licentiate's subjects if the professional intends to work in a role that does not cover their professional competences.

2.3.3 PROVISIONAL MEASURE No. **746/16** – NEW SECONDARY EDUCATION

On 22 September 2016, the current president of Brazil, Michel Temer, and the Minister of Education, Mendonça Filho, announced "the New High School", under Provisional Measure No. 746/16. The biggest change in education in the last 20 years, since the LDB (1996). With a focus on student learning, keeping young people in school and offering a curriculum that meets not only students' individual needs, the proposal also offers opportunities on a par with the world's leading countries (MEC, 2016).

Minister Mendonça Filho justified the change as follows: "Today, around 80% of our young people who finish high school don't go on to college and leave without training for the world of work. We need to give these young people opportunities.

Mendonça gave examples of such actions that have been successful in Brazil:

> Pernambuco now has more than 40 per cent of its secondary school network working full-time and has jumped from 21st place in the Basic Education Development Index (IDEB) in 2007 to first place in the latest results released in 2015. These successful experiences, with concrete and consistent results, show a path for secondary education that is worth following. (MEC, 2016).

The aim of the reform is to prevent school drop-outs and improve the quality of teaching. With the new proposal, the workload will increase from 800 to 1,400 hours, requiring a full shift.

According to the MEC Portal (2016), in the New High School, some subjects will be compulsory during the three years of high school. The other subjects in the Common Base may be taught as determined by the networks and the schools themselves.

Article 36 of Provisional Measure 746/16, which establishes the New High School, states:

> Art. 36: The secondary school curriculum will be made up of the National Common Curriculum Base and specific training itineraries, to be defined by the education systems, with an emphasis on the following areas of knowledge or professional activity:
> I - languages;
> II - maths;
> III - natural sciences;
> IV - humanities; and
> V - technical and vocational training (BRASIL, 2016).

The curriculum, which currently comprises 13 compulsory subjects, will undergo changes. From 2018 it will have more flexibility to prioritise subjects that are of interest to students for future technical or higher education. (MEC, 2016).

Among the subjects that will no longer be compulsory are Arts, Physical Education, Philosophy and Sociology. The aim, according to the federal government, is to encourage schools to offer students the chance to emphasise one of these five areas. Paragraph 3 of Article 26 of Provisional

Measure 746/16 states: "Physical education, integrated into the school's pedagogical proposal, is a compulsory curricular component of early childhood education and primary education, and its practice is optional for the student."

Minister Mendonça Filho (MEC, 2016) said that the central idea of the new change is to give young people "curricular options" and not "curricular impositions". The most important basic requirement, in addition to the common part of the National Curriculum Base, is the demand for a practical component, in the form of supervised activities carried out in the productive sector or in simulation environments.

The proposal has caused disagreement and even outrage on social media. Physical education teachers in particular do not accept "letting the student choose" whether or not to take a physical education class and believe that this new model could further jeopardise the quality of health of the Brazilian population.

CHAPTER 3

METHODOLOGICAL FRAMEWORK

3.1 FOCUS, TYPE OF RESEARCH

The main focus of this study was to find out how accessibility occurs for students with disabilities in Physical Education classes at municipal schools in Caldas Novas-GO.

A mixed study was used to describe and analyse the data obtained. In addition, numerical data was collected on the number of Physical Education teachers and students with disabilities enrolled in municipal schools in the city of Caldas Novas-GO.

3.3 TIME AND SPACE DELIMITATION

The time and space in which the field research was carried out is explained here. The data will be collected from August 2016 to December 2016, a period that is considered sufficient to investigate all the schools in the municipality. The location was chosen as the municipal schools in the city of Caldas Novas, Goiás, Brazil.

3.4 POPULATION AND SAMPLE

Teachers from the municipal education network, school managers and parents or carers of students with disabilities.

According to Lakatos and Marconi (2003, p. 163), "The sample is a conveniently selected portion of the universe (population); it is a subset of the universe.".

People who are directly involved in Physical Education activities in schools and who could give a clear answer about the accessibility of disabled students in these classes will be included. In order to be considered "disabled", the criterion established was that the students had a medical or clinical report describing their disability.

The sample was limited to Physical Education teachers from municipal schools in Caldas Novas-GO who have students with disabilities enrolled. In addition to them, the coordinator of the school surveyed and the legal guardians (parents) of these students.

3.6 HYPOTHESIS

The hypothesis is that PE teachers are not fully prepared to work with students with disabilities. In this way, they miss the opportunity to promote integration between students and school and social inclusion.

3.7 DATA COLLECTION TECHNIQUES AND INSTRUMENTS

This is the phase of the research carried out in order to gather prior information on the field of interest and involves collecting data from various sources (LAKATOS; MARCONI, 2003).

3.7.1 INTERVIEW

As a data collection technique, the interview is very suitable for obtaining information "about what people know, believe, expect, feel or desire, intend to do, do or have done, as well as about their explanations or reasons for the above" (GIL, 2008, p. 109).

A semi-structured interview was carried out with the parents of students with disabilities enrolled in the municipal school system, in order to find out how they are included in Physical

Education activities.

3.7.2 QUESTIONNAIRE

According to Lakatos and Marconi (2003, p. 21), a "questionnaire is a data collection instrument consisting of an ordered series of questions that must be answered in writing and without the presence of the interviewer".

A questionnaire containing closed and open questions was also administered to PE teachers and school coordinators. This was done in order to understand the accessibility of this subject for students with disabilities.

3.8 SOURCES OF INFORMATION

This is the phase of the research carried out with the aim of gathering prior information on the field of interest. According to Lakatos and Marconi (2003, p. 174), data collection should be the first step in any scientific research, and is carried out in two ways "[...] documentary research (or primary sources) and bibliographical research (or secondary sources)".

3.8.1 PRIMARY SOURCES-SUBJECTS

Primary sources are those compiled by the author at the time. In this case, the questionnaire applied to PE teachers and the coordinator of the school where the author works. In addition to the interview conducted with the parents of students with disabilities enrolled in the schools where the research was carried out.

3.8.2 SECONDARY SOURCES-OBJECTS

The secondary sources used are contemporary works such as: Books, Articles, Monographs, Theses, Texts available on the Internet, databases, newspapers, magazines, films, among others that deal with the accessibility of students with disabilities in Physical Education classes.

3.9 HOW THE DATA COLLECTED WAS PROCESSED

The data collected was analysed using graphs for numerical data and descriptively for data containing the opinions and ideas of the interviewees in particular.

3.10 ETHICAL CONSIDERATIONS

The interviewees' real names were not used to preserve their identity. For this purpose, we have used enumerations when referring to the schools, and alphabet letters when referring to the teachers. The coordinators and students' parents will not be quoted directly either.

CHAPTER 4

ANALYTICAL FRAMEWORK

4.1 OBSERVATIONS MADE

The municipality of Caldas Novas, state of Goiás - Brazil, according to the Brazilian Institute of Geography and Statistics - IBGE (2016) has a population of approximately 83,220 inhabitants. According to the Regional Electoral Court of Goiás - TREGO, there are around 48,242 registered voters in Caldas Novas.

It is known for being the largest hydrothermal resort in the world. It has waters that flow from the ground at temperatures ranging from 43° to 70°. For this reason, the town's main source of income is tourism. In high season, such as Carnival, the town can accommodate more than 500,000 tourists from all over the world.

Albuquerque (1996) says that at the time, it was rumoured that Martinho's dogs were chasing a deer when they fell into very hot water, making a lot of noise and attracting Martinho's attention.

It is estimated that more than 3 million tourists visit Caldas Novas every year. Its facilities include hotels, inns, chalets, clubs, discos and bars. It is also located on the banks of the Corumbá River reservoir and next to the Serra de Caldas mountain range.

Caldas Novas was discovered in 1722 by Bartolomeu Bueno da Silva. Initially it belonged to the Santa Cruz region, in the Goiás hinterland. Martinho Coelho de Siqueira led a movement to create a town to exploit its hot springs in 1777. It was politically emancipated on 21 October 1911 (ALBUQUERQUE, 1996).

Its waters are renowned for their therapeutic properties. The first private spa was founded in 1910 by Major Victor de Ozeda Ala (ALBUQUERQUE, 1996, p.28). The wooden bathhouse, with two bathtubs, currently serves as the Municipal Spa and is visited by tourists on a daily basis.

According to Albuquerque (1996), the first school in Caldas Novas was created in 1870, with master Limírio Ribeiro Quinta as its teacher. Currently, according to IBGE data (2015), there are 11,976 students enrolled, divided between municipal and public schools. In the municipality there are 6,184 enrolled in primary school.

Our study focused on the 18 municipal schools, with the exception of school number 5 in Table 1, which is a school for specialised care for people with disabilities and does not provide regular primary education. So that leaves 17 schools surveyed.

Table 1 - List of Municipal Schools in Caldas Novas-GO

N°	SCHOOLS	NEIGHBOURHOOD
1	Dona Abelina Municipal School	Boa Vista Resort
2	Edith Ala Municipal School	Breeze Park
3	Feliciano Ivo Municipal School	Jardim Paraíso II
4	Felipe Marinho Municipal School	Jequitimar
5	Hélia Rodrigues Municipal School	New Town
6	Limírio Rosa Municipal School	Holliday
7	Mather Isabel Municipal School	St Joseph
8	Norbeto Odebrecht Municipal School	Hot Water Mansions
9	Orlando Rodrigues Municipal School	Itaguaí II
10	Orozina Maria Municipal School	Serrano Garden
11	Celina Belo Municipal School	Holliday
12	Professor Zico Batista Municipal School	Royal Park
13	Reginaldo Ríspole Municipal School	Jardim Brasil
14	Santa Efigênia Municipal School	Santa Efigênia
15	Valdir Arantes Municipal School	University Sector
16	Geraldo Dias Municipal School	Grupinho village
17	Waldomiro G. de Sousa Municipal School	Sapé village
18	Youth and Adult Education	St Joseph

Source: Organised by the author (2017).

The municipal schools in Caldas Novas-GO cater for pupils from the age of 6, who are in the first year of primary school, to those in secondary school. In addition to school number 18, which caters for young people and adults in the EJA system[1] .

Some of these schools operate in the morning or afternoon, others full time (morning and afternoon) and others also offer evening classes.

There are 529 teachers in the city, 241 of whom are working in primary education, in the schools listed above. Of these professionals, 20 are Physical Education teachers working in the municipality.

4.2 ANALYSING RESEARCH DATA

As explained in Chapter III, which describes the Methodological Framework, the data collection techniques and instruments used for the field research were the questionnaire applied to the teachers and coordinators of the field schools, and the interview conducted with the parents of students with disabilities.

4.2.1 PHYSICAL EDUCATION TEACHERS

We endeavoured to list all the Physical Education teachers in the municipality of Caldas Novas. It can be seen that all of the city's teachers have a degree in Physical Education, whether it's a bachelor's degree, graduate degree or school degree.

According to the municipality's general coordinator for Physical Education, this basic training is a prerequisite for entry into municipal public tenders. According to him, everyone who works in this area is a civil servant and there are no contracts for this position.

In order to better visualise the 20 Physical Education teachers and preserve their identity, their names, in abbreviations, and their degrees were listed at random. See Table 2.

It's worth noting that the acronyms that are highlighted in the same colour refer to teachers who work in two schools.

Table 2 - Physical education teachers and their training

N°	PROF. ED. TEACHER			GRADUATION
1	C. A.	C. S.		Physical Ed.
2	H. L.	L. P.		Degree in Phys. Ed. and Phys. Ed.
3	F. T.			Degree in Physical Education
4	M. M.			Degree in Physical Education
5	T. P.			Degree in Physical Education
6	C. A.	H. A.		Physical Education School
7	C. N.			Physical Ed.
8	N. T.			Degree in Physical Education
9	**A.U.**			Bachelor of Physical Education
10	J. R.			Physical Ed.
11	J. M.			Degree in Physical Education
12	L. V.			Degree in Physical Education
13	K. F.	R. M.	H. A|	Physical Education and School Physical Education School
14	C. S.			Bachelor of Physical Education
15	C. N.			Physical Ed.
16	J. R.			Physical Education School
17	P. Q.	**A.U**	T. P|	Phys. Ed. and Licentiate in Phys. Ed.

Source: Organised by the author (2017).

Table 2 also shows that the term "Physical Education" is highlighted in yellow. It's worth pointing out that this was done to emphasise that when the teachers were interviewed, they said that

[1]This type of education was born out of a clear need to offer a better chance to people who, for whatever reason, did not finish primary and/or secondary school at the appropriate age.

they had a degree in Physical Education, which covers both the educational and other areas. According to them, they can work both in schools and gyms.

However, from the research carried out on the subject, in chapter "2.3 LEGAL FRAMEWORK", it was possible to see that Physical Education teachers must either have a Bachelor's degree or a Licentiate degree, because the curricular matrix that permeates these courses is different from each other. Regarding this, the coordinator said: "I can't tell you that there is a document in the municipality that forbids a bachelor's degree in Physical Education from being in the classroom".

With regard to postgraduate qualifications, it was possible to see that not all teachers have them. There were 9 who had a postgraduate degree, 8 who didn't and 3 who said they were studying. None of them has a Master's degree.

As for the areas in which the teachers completed their postgraduate programmes, they include: Higher Education Teaching, Exercise Physiology, Yoga, Physiotherapy and Sports Management. However, none of them covered the areas of primary education, special education or inclusion. One of the interviewees said: "I'd like to study 'Adapted Physical Activity and Health', but unfortunately there aren't any in the region".

With regard to gender, there is a predominance of males in the physical education profession, as can be seen in Graph 1 below.

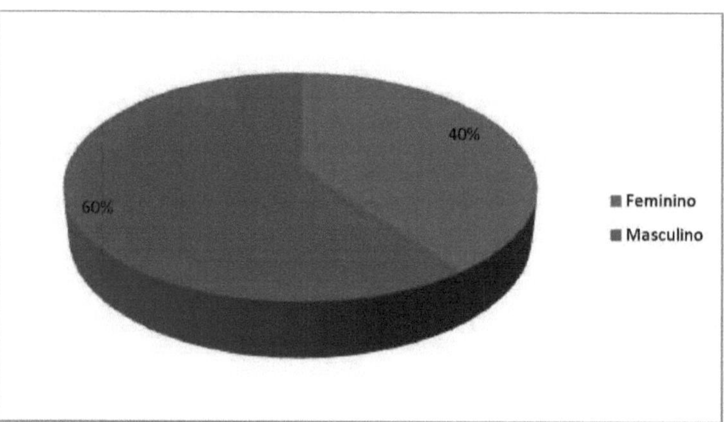

Graph 1 - Sex of PE teachers
Source: Organised by the author (2017).

Question 2 of the questionnaire applied to teachers sought to find out their age. The result can be seen in Graph 2.

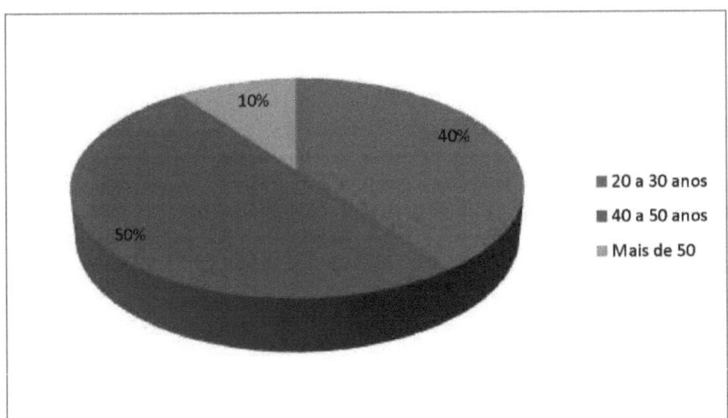

Graph 2 - Age of PE teachers
Source: Organised by the author (2017).

It can be seen that the majority, totalling 50% of PE teachers, are aged between 40 and 50. Another 40 per cent are aged between 20 and 30. Only 10 per cent of the 20 teachers are over 50.

We tried to find out how many students with disabilities the teachers cater for. The teachers differed greatly from the data collected from the coordinator (TABLE 3). The majority reported having between 1 and 5 special needs students. However, the table shows that there are schools with 6, 7, 11 and even 14 students with disabilities.

This discrepancy could be due to the fact that the teachers don't understand exactly what a disability is, due to a lack of knowledge in the area of Special Education. Or there may be a lack of communication between the school coordinator and the PE teacher.

Graph 3 shows the results of question 5, which asked: "Do they have a diagnosis or report?".

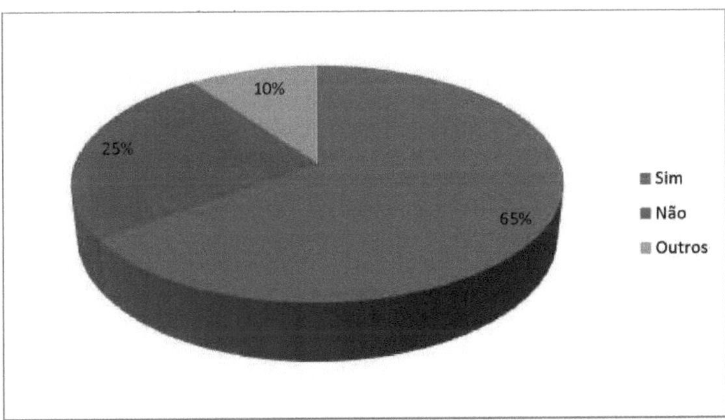

Graph 3 - Students with a medical certificate
Source: Organised by the author (2017).

It can be seen that 65 per cent of teachers said that their disabled student(s) had a medical report or a diagnosis of their physical, cognitive or psychological conditions. A further 25 per cent said "No".

A further 10 per cent chose "Other" and justified their choice as follows:

"I know it looks like he has a report, but I can't say because I've never seen it."

23

(TEACHER I).

"Although his disability is very visible, I've never been curious enough to ask for a report." (TEACHER II).

It was possible to see that the teachers, despite knowing that their student has a certain disability, did not have access to the document that diagnoses it. Once again, this shows the lack of communication between teachers and the school's coordination team. Only one of the teachers who ticked "Yes" explained that he had access to the child's report through his parents.

With this in mind, we asked the PE teachers if they had had access to this student's documents, either from their parents or from the school office. Graph 4 shows the results of this question.

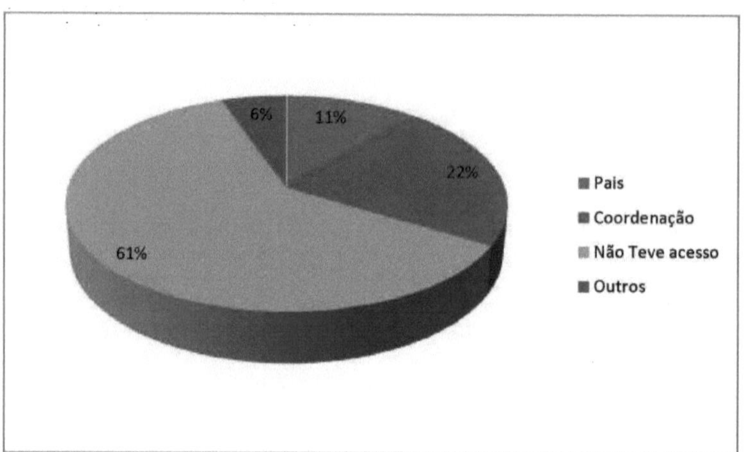

Graph 4 - Access to student reports
Source: Organised by the author (2017).

It can be seen that 61 per cent of the interviewees said that they did not have access to the reports describing their student's disability. A further 22 per cent said they had access to these documents through the school's coordination and 11 per cent said it was through the parents.

Only one teacher, totalling 6%, represented in Graph 4, chose the "Other" option. He described that "Because my student has Dow Syndrome and it's a very visible disability, I don't think a report is necessary. We already know what to do and how to work with these children."

In question 7, PE teachers were asked: "Have you ever received training courses to work with students with disabilities?". The results of the answers can be seen in Graph 5.

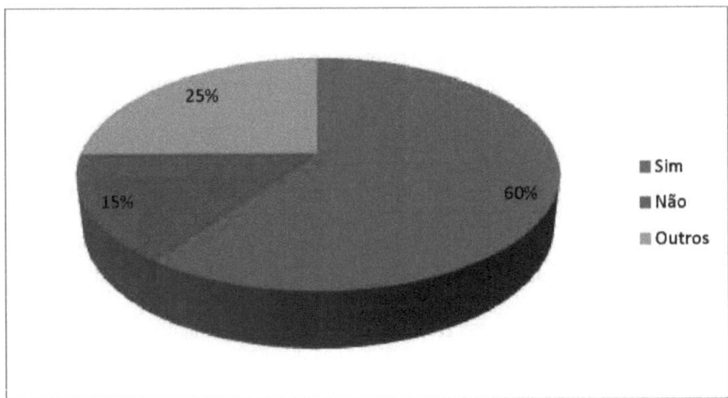

Graph 5 - Training courses offered to teachers

When asked about their continuing education, with training courses in the area of Special Education and School Inclusion, the majority, totalling 60% of teachers, said "Yes", while 15% said "No".

25% of the teachers chose the "Other" option, and one of them gave the following reason: "We receive lectures from the municipality when there is a teachers' meeting. Not really courses.

It is understood that becoming a teacher is a long-term process of new learning with no fixed end. In this way, the continuous or ongoing training of this professional contributes significantly to the development of: the teacher's professional knowledge; their ability to reflect on their own teaching practice; the processes of change and the consequences this has for the educational environment.

Silva, Sousa and Vidal (2008) in their research reported that the biggest problem reported by the teachers themselves was the lack of more adequate training (initial and continuing), which is a determining factor in the fact that pedagogical actions are not satisfactory when working with students who have special educational needs in the same space as those who are "normal".

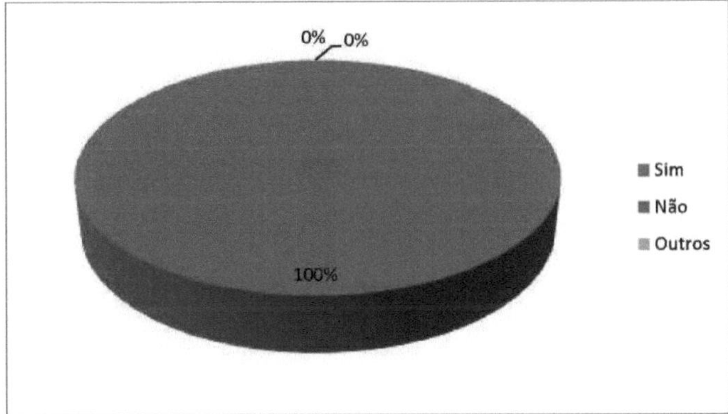

Graph 6 - Disabled students' participation in lessons

Question 8 asked the following question: "Do your student(s) regularly attend Physical Education classes?". See Graph 6 on the previous page for the results. It can be seen that the teachers were unanimous in stating that their students with disabilities regularly attend PE classes.

There were the following written reports: "I have one who misses a lot, because he only comes to class when he's well, but he's a regular student, he participates normally.". (TEACHER III). "She's only absent when she's ill or has her period, because her mum prefers her to stay at home on those days". (TEACHER IV). "He goes to Goiânia right, so he misses a lot, but when he comes to class and it's a PE day, he takes part normally." (TEACHER V).

As reported in the theoretical framework of this study, one of the aims of Physical Education classes is to provide opportunities to value differences, be they physical, ethnic, cultural, religious or gender. It is understood that in this way it is possible to eliminate any barrier and any type of discrimination.

It is therefore understood that the Physical Education teacher has the opportunity to show the school that being different is normal, because, after all, everyone is different from each other in at least one characteristic.

We then sought to find out from the PE teacher how the disabled student relates to other classmates. Graph 7 shows the results of this question.

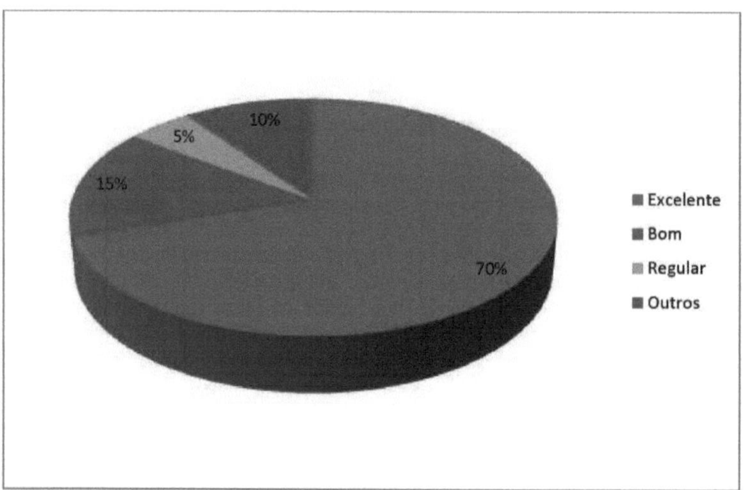

Graph 7 - Relationship with other colleagues
Source: Organised by the author (2017).

Graph 7 shows that the majority of PE teachers at municipal schools in the city of Caldas Novas-GO stated that the relationship between their disabled student(s) and other colleagues was "Excellent". 15% described this relationship as good and 5% as regular.

Another 10 per cent described the following:

> "We've already had problems with him because of his aggressive behaviour. It seems that the doctor changed the medication he was taking before for another one, but today he's calmer. The boys love to call him to play football". (TEACHER VI).
> **"When it comes to playing, he can't accept losing and many times he's taken the ball and** ended the game. So some of his classmates find it hard to accept and understand **his behaviour." (TEACHER VII).**

It can be seen that PE teachers encounter behavioural problems in relation to students with disabilities during their lessons. It is not known for sure how they have dealt with this situation, but this is a question that could be addressed in further research.

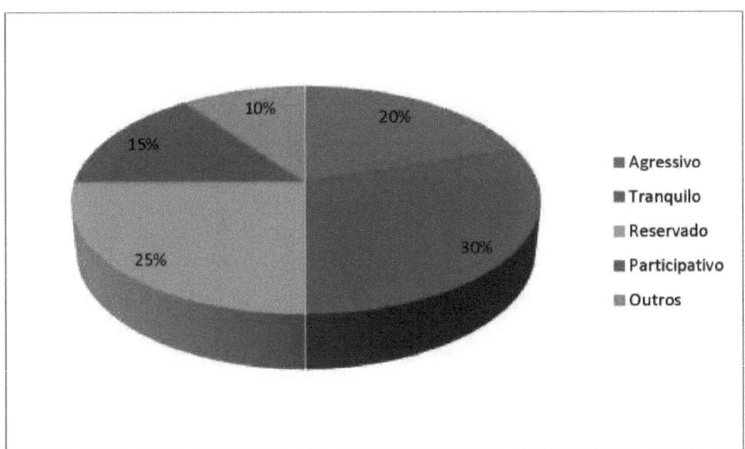

Graph 8 - Behaviour of students with disabilities
Source: Organised by the author (2017).

Graph 8 shows questions related to this student's behaviour during PE lessons. The caption lists the adjectives most used by the teachers to give their answer.

So, 30% of teachers consider the behaviour of their disabled student to be "Quiet", another 25% consider him to be "Reserved", 15% believe him to be "Participative".

However, 20% reported that their student's behaviour was "Aggressive" and 10% ticked the "Other" box. Once again, the issue of aggression came to the fore in this survey. This is due to the fact that many of the disabilities cited by teachers are related to children who have (Mental Retardation, Hyperactivity, Schizophrenia or Mental Disability).

Mantoan (2003) says that aggression in children is one of the most difficult situations to deal with, especially because it stirs up the instincts of adults, who also react almost instinctively. The feeling of frustration is great. It follows that teacher training should also cover this issue.

The graph on the next page, Graph 9, shows the following question put to PE teachers: "Do you believe that what you work on/teach has helped your (disabled) student to have a more acceptable attitude towards health concerns?".

On this question, 80 per cent of the teachers answered "Yes", their students, even with disabilities, are capable of learning and show concern for their health.

Another 5 per cent answered "No". Two PE teachers from the same school said that his disability, "cerebral palsy", was serious and that he was "out of it". This means that the student shows no interest in maintaining a good diet or in the results of physical activities. According to them "[...] he just wants to play".

Graph 9 also shows that 15% of the teachers who answered the questionnaire ticked the "Other" box. One of their justifications is described here: "I can't say that he's concerned about his health, but I do know that he understands that eating pizza, for example, makes you fat and that it's better to eat fruit". (TEACHER IV).

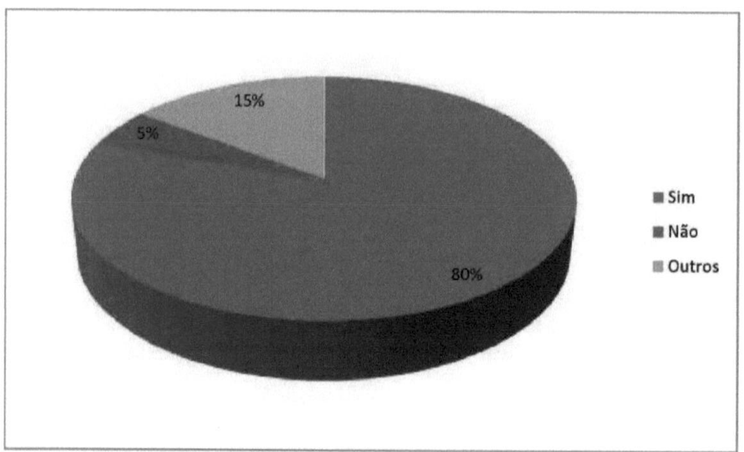

Graph 9 - Students with disabilities and health concerns
Source: Organised by the author (2017).

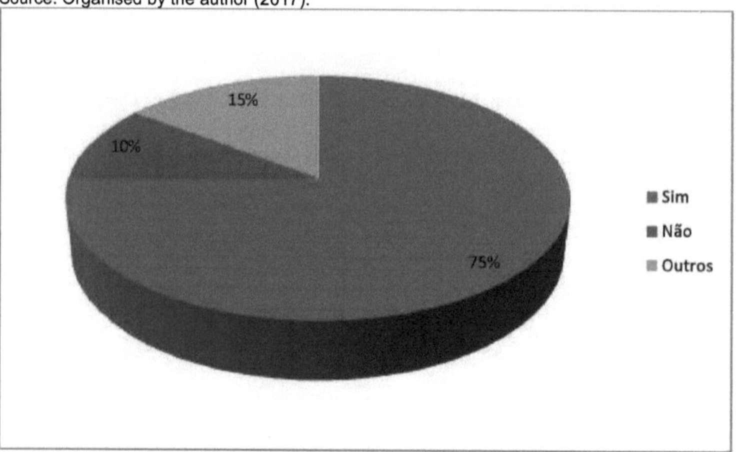

Graph 10 - Parents' concern about their child's development
Source: Organised by the author (2017).

We also sought to find out from PE teachers in the municipality of Caldas Novas-GO whether the parents of students with disabilities are concerned about their son or daughter's motor/physical development.

This question can be seen in Graph 10 on the previous page. It can be seen that 75% of teachers believe that parents are concerned about their child's physical and/or motor development. However, 10 per cent said that parents do not have this concern.

One of the teachers who answered "No" reported that the child needs intensive treatment at the physiotherapist and that the hand doesn't take the child even after the school has obtained this free care from the town hall.

Graph 10 also shows that 15% of teachers ticked the "Other" box. The teachers said they couldn't say whether or not parents were concerned about their child's physical development. However, they said that "at school" they never received parents with this kind of concern.

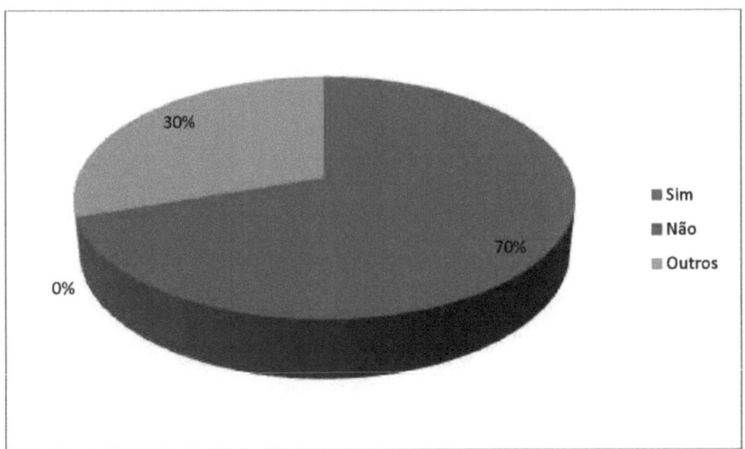

Graph 11 - Activity adapted for students with disabilities
Source: Organised by the author (2017).

In question 13, the following question was asked: "Have you ever carried out an "adapted" activity so that your student could participate and excel in the activities?". The results are shown in Graph 11 above.

None of the teachers answered "No". 70% of them said that they carry out adapted activities with their class in order to include their disabled student in it.

30 per cent of the teachers ticked the "Other" box and made it clear that they make these adaptations, but that in some classes, when they involve an activity that requires greater physical conditioning, this disabled student is "left out" of the class.

According to the PCNs (1997), physical education lessons don't have to be structured according to these students (with disabilities), but the teacher can be flexible, making the necessary adjustments. It is possible to integrate these children into the group, respecting their limitations and, at the same time, giving them the opportunity to develop their potential.

In question 14, PE teachers were asked to explain what adaptations they made during their lessons to meet the physical needs of their students with disabilities.

The teachers listed various adaptations that they had already made:
1. Longer warm-up;
2. Games that develop motor skills;

3. Recreational games;
4. Wheelchair picnic;
5. Shuttlecock game;
6. Wheel games;
7. Game of biloca (marbles);
8. Hot Potato Game;
9. Corporal of war sitting on the ground;
10. Basketball with a lower basket;
11. Blind" football;
12. Run with both legs (one of each partner) tied together;
13. Hit the target with paper balls;
14. Bowling;
15. Dance;
16. Theatre;
17. Articulated doll;

29

18. Pass pet bottle balls;
19. Pet bottle shuttle;
20. Rod;
21. Dominoes and checkers;
22. What's that sound?
23. Smell the odour;
24. Ring game.

The teacher has to innovate and diversify, because the field of work involves many activities that can be worked on with students, such as games, competitions, dance, music, theatre, body expression, physical fitness practices, mime games, gymkhanas, reading texts, written and practical work, group dynamics, the use of TV, DVDs and so on.

As Rodrigues (2013) says, the field is very broad. All it takes is for the teacher to be responsible, serious and creative. A job well done should encourage longevity with quality.

According to Miquelin and Fernandes (2014), unfortunately many PE teachers still waste class time by giving students a ball to play football, volleyball or whatever they think is best.

The authors also point out that many professionals today are not concerned with motivating their students. They don't plan their lessons and don't have a predetermined objective or purpose for the lesson. It should be realised that Physical Education is not just about running, playing games, playing ball or doing gymnastics.

4.2.2 COORDINATORS OF THE SCHOOLS SURVEYED

In view of the 17 schools in the municipality of Caldas Novas-GO, and after applying a questionnaire to the Physical Education teachers in each of them, it was necessary to find out the coordinators' opinion of the work of these teachers and, in turn, to understand the accessibility offered to students with disabilities by this school management.

The first question of the questionnaire applied to the coordinators sought to find out the gender of the coordinators who were answering the questionnaire.

Graph 12 shows that 71 per cent of coordinators are female, while 29 per cent are male. It can be seen that while Physical Education is mostly taught by men, school coordination is mostly done by women.

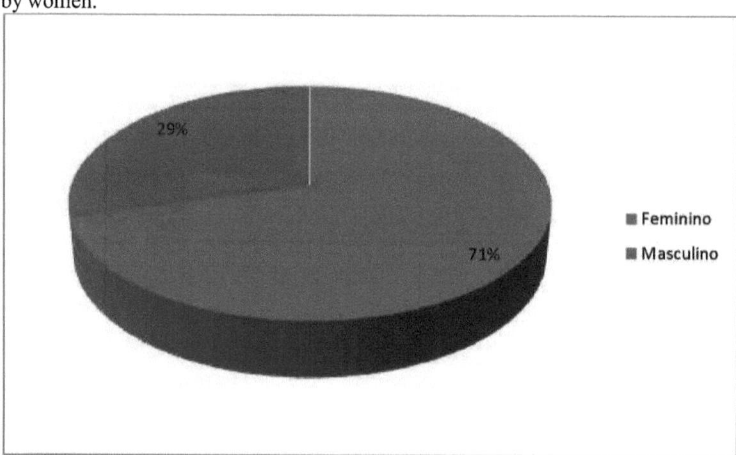

Graph 12 - Sex of coordinators
Source: Organised by the author (2017).

The age of these coordinators, who are in charge of decisions made within the school environment, was also the focus of this research, in question 2.

Graph 13 shows that the majority of these educational managers are aged between 40 and 50, totalling 59%. Followed by 29 per cent aged between 20 and 30, only 12 per cent are over 60.

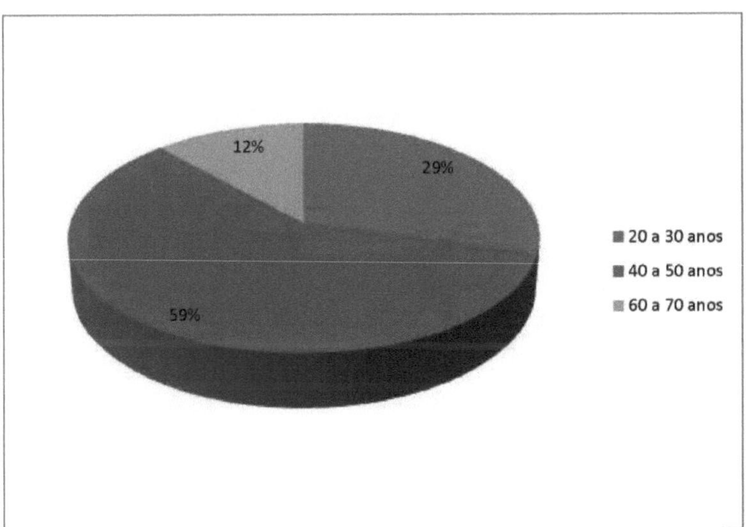

Graph 13 - Age of coordinators
Source: Organised by the author (2017).

As for the coordinators' academic backgrounds, we sought to find out their degrees, specialisations and other higher or complementary education.

Graph 14 shows that both coordinators have a degree, which is one of the requirements for the position they occupy. 47% of them have a degree in Pedagogy, 17% in Biology and 12% in Languages. Geography, Maths and History both account for 6% of the data.

It's worth noting here that one of the coordinators interviewed has a degree in Physical Education (he didn't say whether it's a degree or a bachelor's), which is the focus of this field research.

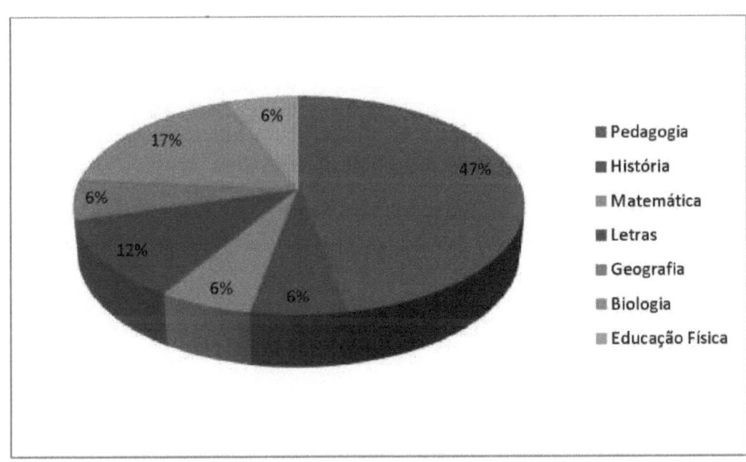

Graph 14 - Coordinators' degrees
Source: Organised by the author (2017).

Graph 15 shows the specialisation and other training that these coordinators have: 47% of the interviewees have some kind of specialisation, while 17% have none.

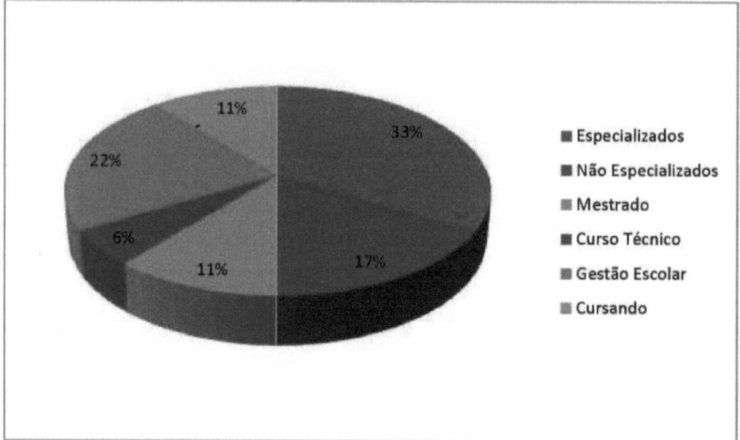

Graph 15 - Specialisation and other training
Source: Organised by the author (2017).

It can be seen that 22% of the coordinators have a specialisation in School or Educational Management. 11% of them reported that they were studying for a specialisation, but did not say which area they were studying in.

Graph 15 also shows that 11 per cent of the interviewees reported having completed a Master's degree. And 6 per cent of the coordinators said that they had completed a technical course in addition to their undergraduate degree.

One of them is a computer technician and another, a little outside of education, a nursing technician.

Question 4 asked: "How many students with disabilities does the school currently have?". It's worth emphasising here that we only wanted to know about those students who have a diagnosed disability and who have a medical or clinical report to prove their pedagogical needs.

The Aurélio dictionary (FERREIRA, 2004) defines the word "disability" as a term used to define the absence or dysfunction of a psychic, physiological or anatomical structure. The LDB (1996) describes it as disability (without specifications), global development disorder and giftedness or high abilities. Law No. 12.764/12 added Autism as "I - persistent and clinically significant impairment of social communication and interaction, manifested by marked impairment of verbal and non-verbal communication".

There was a wide variety in the coordinators' responses regarding the number of students with disabilities enrolled in the school they coordinate, and in order to better organise them, Table 3 below was used.

Table 3 - Number of students with disabilities per school

N°	SCHOOLS	STUDENTS WITH DISABILITIES
1	Dona Abelina Municipal School	02 students
2	Edith Ala Municipal School	14 students
3	Feliciano Ivo Municipal School	01 student
4	Felipe Marinho Municipal School	01 students
5	Hélia Rodrigues Municipal School	He didn't take part.

6	Limírio Rosa Municipal School	06 students
7	Mather Isabel Municipal School	11 students
8	Norbeto Odebrecht Municipal School	05 students
9	Orlando Rodrigues Municipal School	07 students
10	Orozina Maria Municipal School	01 student
11	Celina Belo Municipal School	03 students
12	Professor Zico Batista Municipal School	02 students
13	Reginaldo Ríspole Municipal School	04 students
14	Santa Efigênia Municipal School	01 student
15	Valdir Arantes Municipal School	01 student
16	Geraldo Dias Municipal School	05 students
17	Waldomiro G. de Sousa Municipal School	02 students
18	Youth and Adult Education	02 students

Source: Organised by the author (2017).

The coordinators listed 68 students diagnosed with some kind of disability. Among the schools with the highest number of students, Edith Ala Municipal School had 14 students with diagnoses, and Mather Isabel Municipal School had 11 children with diagnoses.

Question 5 asked whether all students with disabilities take part in the activities proposed in PE lessons.

Graph 16 shows that the coordinators unanimously stated that all these students attend classes normally.

One of the coordinators ticked the "Other" box, totalling 6%, and explained that the student he was referring to has "Cerebral Palsy", uses wheelchairs and his mobility is very limited. So he is present in all PE lessons, but doesn't take part in all the activities.

She also reported that the student's mother accompanies him to school, taking him to the toilet, to the playground and to PE class. And when there are activities that he can take part in, she sits and watches him "have fun". According to the coordinator, there are medical restrictions on some body movements.

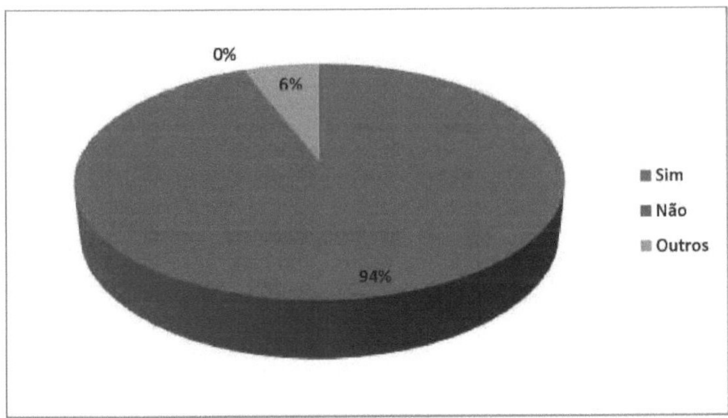

Graph 16 - Students who take part in PE lessons
Source: Organised by the author (2017).

In question 6, the coordinators were asked how they assessed the work of the PE teacher with students with disabilities.

Graph 17 shows that 88 per cent of coordinators rate the work of their PE teachers as "Excellent" and only 6 per cent rate it as "Good".

Only one of the coordinators surveyed ticked the "Other" box and explained that the teacher is a recent graduate and still needs time to adapt to the educational and inclusive reality.

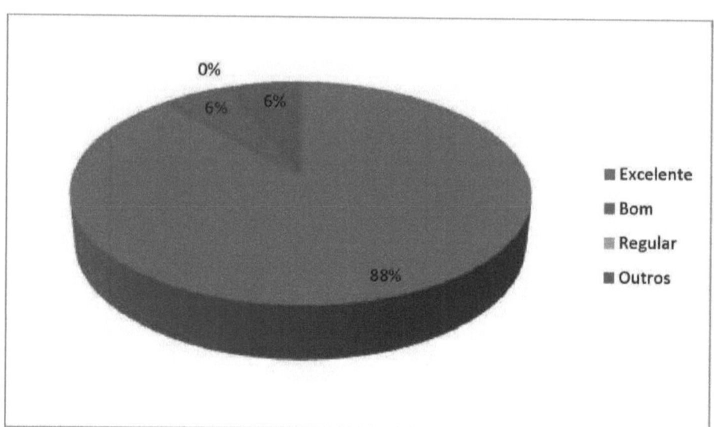

Graph 17 - Evaluation of the physical education teacher's work
Source: Organised by the author (2017).

I also asked the coordinator if the municipality of Caldas Novas-GO has offered or is offering any kind of training for Physical Education teachers to enable them to cater for students with disabilities.

The coordinators, totalling 82%, according to Graph 18, said that the municipality of Caldas Novas-GO offers courses to train PE teachers to deal with disabilities in their classes.

One of the coordinators said: "It's offered in conjunction with the other teachers, not specifically for the PE teacher". (COORDINATOR 1).

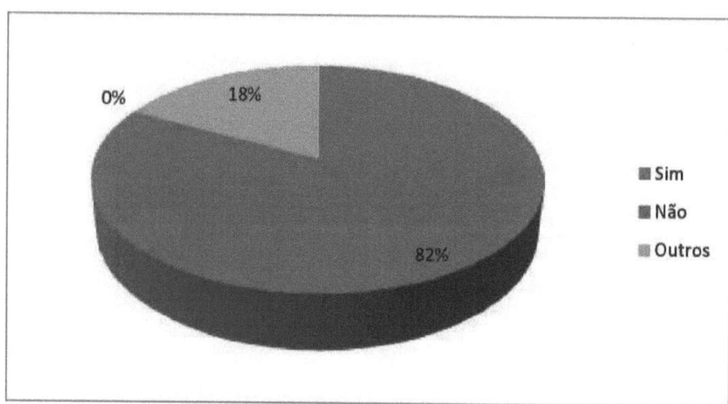

Graph 18 - Training offered by the municipality
Source: Organised by the author (2017).

Still on Graph 18, three of the interviewees ticked the "Other" box and gave their reasons:

"Yes, but in general. They don't address all the deficiencies we have **here. In this case, the teacher has to seek knowledge on their own."** (COORDINATOR 2).

"I know that the municipality has already offered it, but it's not common practice. Last year, when I took over as coordinator, I'm sure there was **nothing about it." (COORDINATOR 3).**

The same question was asked of Physical Education teachers, but 25% (No) and 15% (Other), totalling 40%, said that the municipality does not offer this specific training.

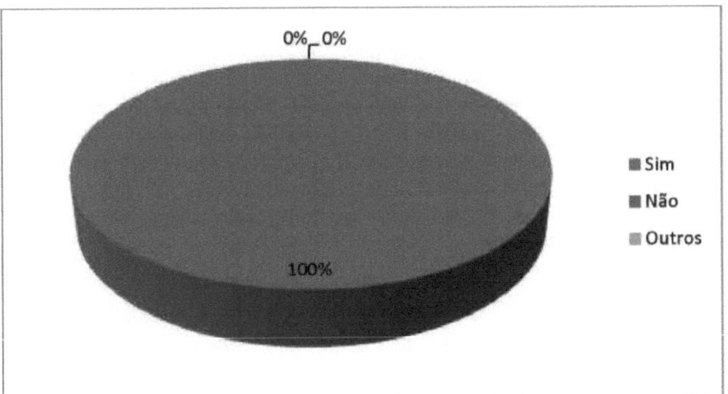

Graph 19 - Importance of Physical Education for students with disabilities
Source: Organised by the author (2017).

Question 8 asked the coordinator if he believed that Physical Education was important for students with disabilities.

Graph 19 shows that once again the coordinators' responses were unanimous, as all of them answered "Yes".

Question 9 asked the following question: "Do you notice any concern on the part of parents regarding the participation of their children with disabilities in PE lessons?".

Graph 20 shows that 70% of the coordinators answered "No" and 18% answered "Yes". This discrepancy is justified by the fact that many disabilities do not require specific care in terms of mobility or physical activity.

12% of the interviewees ticked "Other" when describing their parents' concerns about PE lessons (GRAPH 20).

One of them explained that there is concern, but that it doesn't go beyond other parents who have children without disabilities.

The other explained that parents worry almost daily, but this is due to the type of disability their child has, which requires special care even during break times.

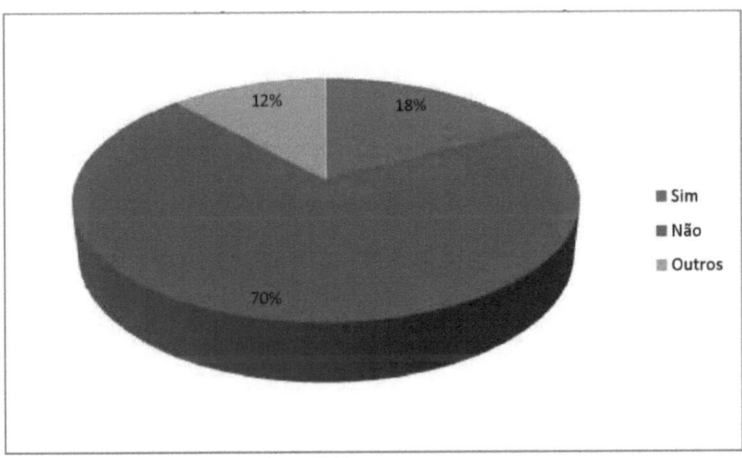

Graph 20 - Parents' concern about PE lessons
Source: Organised by the author (2017).

The question was also asked: "Has the school made any adaptations (furniture, architecture, teaching materials, etc.) to cater for students with disabilities?".

The Aurélio dictionary (FERREIRA, 2004, p.16) explains the term "adaptation" as "a verb that refers to the fact of accommodating or adjusting one thing to another".

According to the LDB (1996), students with disabilities have the right to adaptations in the curriculum, methods, techniques, educational resources and specific organisations to meet their needs. In addition, as described in the theoretical framework, they have the right, according to Art. 59, "III - teachers with appropriate specialisation at secondary or higher level, for specialised care, as well as regular education teachers trained for the integration of these students [...]".

Graph 21 shows that 100 per cent of coordinators say that their school makes some kind of adaptation to accommodate students with disabilities.

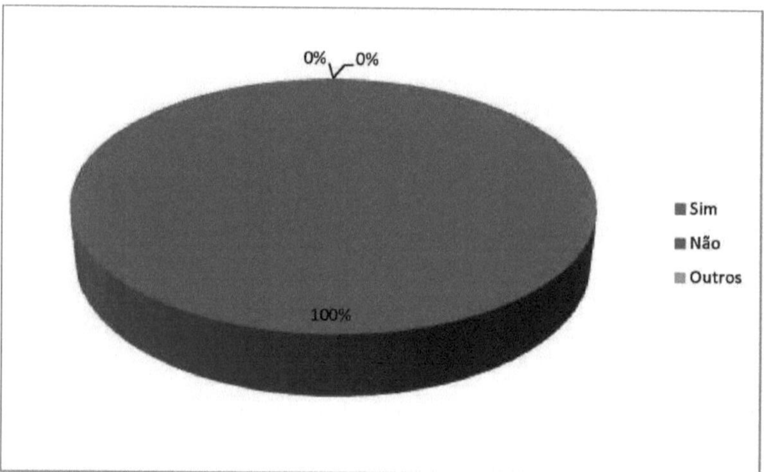

Graph 21 - Adaptations for accessibility
Source: Organised by the author (2017).

Some used the "Other" field to justify that the students they have in their school didn't need "architectural or furniture" adaptations because their disability is cognitive and learning, not physical.

The last question in the questionnaire applied to the coordinators asked whether the school had ever received or had received any students who were unable to take part in PE lessons for any reason.

Graph 22 shows that 71 per cent of the coordinators reported that their school had never received a student with a disability who was banned from taking part in PE lessons. 29 per cent said that they had already received this type of student.

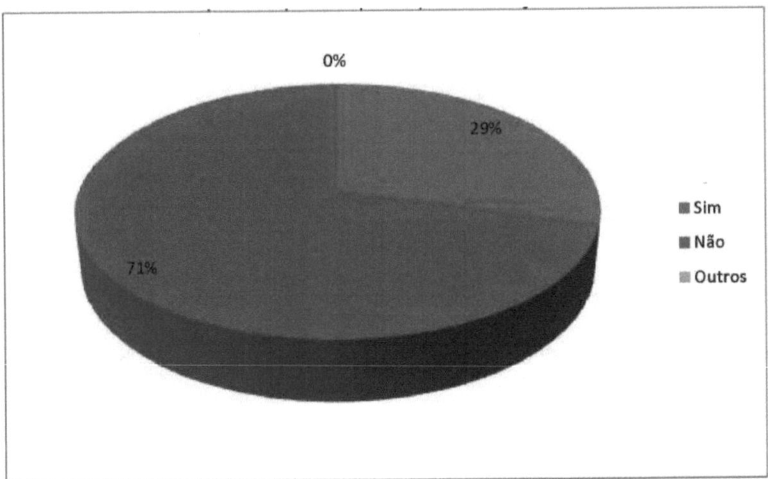

Graph 22 - Students unable to take part in Physical Education
Source: Organised by the author (2017).

Still on Graph 22, it's worth noting that two of the teachers, using the field for justifying their answer, wrote:

> **"We've already had a pupil with a heart condition who couldn't take part in PE lessons." (COORDINATOR 4).**

> **"One of our students uses a 'walker' so there are some activities he doesn't do, like playing volleyball." (COORDINATOR 5).**

It's worth pointing out that most of the disabilities that are present in schools are of a pedagogical, cognitive or learning nature. There are fewer physical disabilities and these are the ones that can prevent students from being present in Physical Education classes.

4.2.3 INTERVIEW WITH THE PARENTS OF STUDENTS WITH DISABILITIES

As 68 students with disabilities were identified in the municipal school system who attend Physical Education classes, the 68 parents were invited to take part in the interview.

The invitation (Appendix E) was adapted according to the reality of the school and the number of students to be interviewed. Not all parents responded. A contingent of 13 parents took part in the interview.

Table 4 shows the number of parents interviewed per school. The rest of the parents either refused to take part in the survey or did not reply during the interview period.

For better quality, absorption and understanding of the answers given by the parents, the interview was conducted with a voice recording, with their authorisation. This made it possible to review the reports and transcribe those that were most relevant.

Table 4 - Number of parents who took part in the interview

N°	SCHOOLS	STUDENTS WITH DISABILITIES	Parents interviewed
1	Dona Abelina Municipal School	02 students	
2	Edith Ala Municipal School	14 students	03 parents
3	Feliciano Ivo Municipal School	01 student	
4	Felipe Marinho Municipal School	01 students	
5	Hélia Rodrigues Municipal School	He didn't take part.	

6	Limírio Rosa Municipal School	06 students	
7	Mather Isabel Municipal School	11 students	04 parents
8	Norbeto Odebrecht Municipal School	05 students	
9	Orlando Rodrigues Municipal School	07 students	01 father
10	Orozina Maria Municipal School	01 student	
11	Celina Belo Municipal School	03 students	01 father
12	Professor Zico Batista Municipal School	02 students	
13	Reginaldo Ríspole Municipal School	04 students	01 father
14	Santa Efigenia Municipal School	01 student	01 father
15	Valdir Arantes Municipal School	01 student	
16	Geraldo Dias Municipal School	05 students	
17	Waldomiro G. de Sousa Municipal School	02 students	2 parents
18	Youth and Adult Education	02 students	

Source: Organised by the author (2017).

This low rate of parents willing to take part in the survey is in line with what Silva, Seabra Júnior and Araújo (2008) warn in their book "Educação

Adapted Physics in Brazil" that the participation of parents in their children's school life is of paramount importance in order to achieve good future results. More than biological characteristics, parents pass on behaviour, values and, above all, attitudes towards life to their children.

On the other hand, Carvalho (1998) argues that the absence or invisibility of parents in the physical space of the school does not necessarily mean lack of interest or disregard for their children's schooling.

As for the sex of the parents who were present for the interview, it is summarised as follows in Graph 23.

It can be seen that the majority of parents interviewed, totalling 85%, are female and only 15% are male.

During the interview, the marital status of the parents was asked. Of the 13 interviewees, 6 were married, 2 were single and 5 were separated or divorced.

One of the male interviewees reported looking after his son on his own. Another who agreed to take part was the paternal grandmother, who said she had custody of her granddaughter since she realised she had been born with a disability (mental handicap).

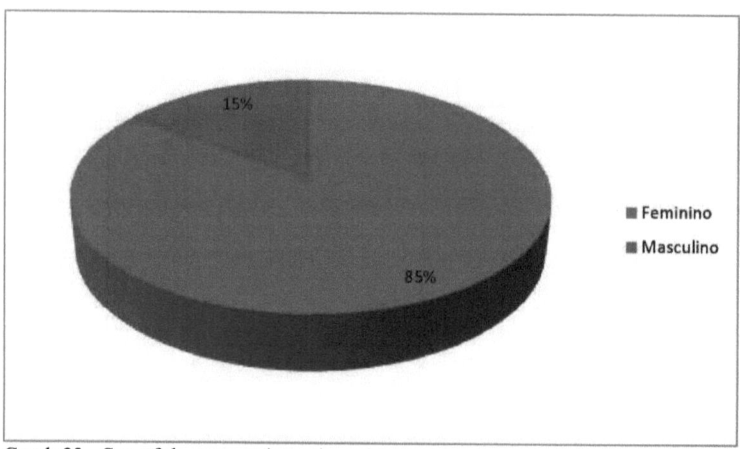

Graph 23 - Sex of the parents interviewed
Source: Organised by the author (2017).

The age of the parents interviewed can be seen in Graph 24. 77 per cent of the parents were aged between 30 and 40. A further 15 per cent are aged between 18 and 20 and 8 per cent are aged between 50 and 60. It's worth noting that the 8 per cent figure refers to the grandmother who is responsible.

Still on Graph 24, one of the younger interviewees is 18 and is not the child's mother. It's her older sister, but she's the one who takes and picks up the student from school every day. She said that she lives three blocks from the school and that she picks up her brother because he is in a wheelchair and needs help crossing the road.

We also sought to find out the academic background of the interviewees, on the understanding that the higher their level of education, the greater their perception of Physical Education classes.

Graph 25 shows that 46 per cent of parents have completed secondary school, 23 per cent have not completed secondary school, 15 per cent have completed primary school, which ranges from 6th to 9th grade, and 8 per cent have completed primary school, which ranges from 1st to 5th grade.

Only one of the interviewees reported having a degree in Business Administration. This low level of education is due to the fact that the majority of students enrolled in municipal schools are children of low-income parents.

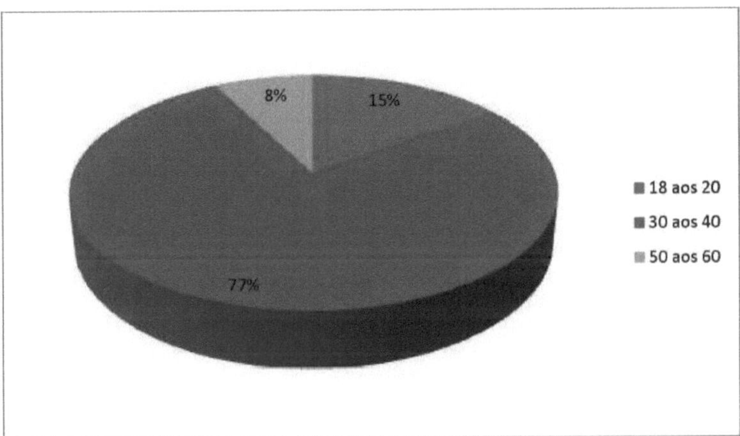

Graph 24 - Age of parents interviewed
Source: Organised by the author (2017).

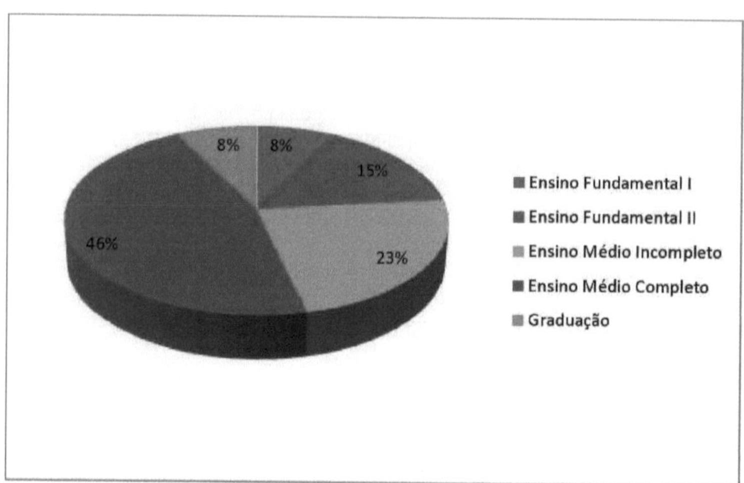

Graph 25 - Educational level of the parents interviewed
Source: Organised by the author (2017).

Question 4 of the interview script asked: "Does your child regularly attend PE lessons?". The answer was as shown in Graph 26.

It can be seen that 86 per cent of the parents interviewed reported that their children regularly take part in PE lessons. None of them chose the "No" option.

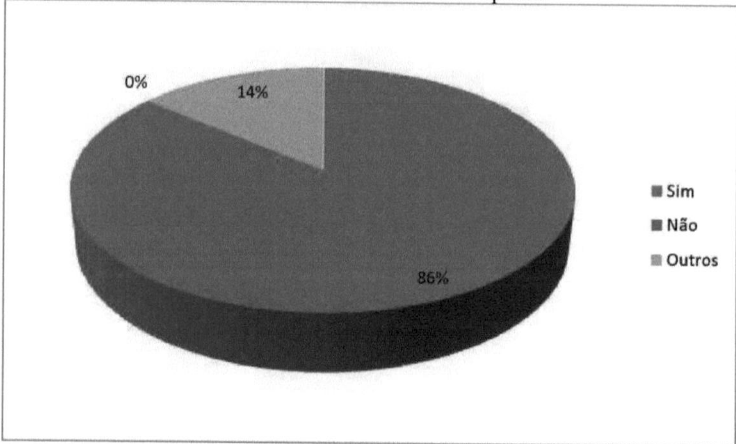

Graph 26 - Students who regularly attend PE lessons
Source: Organised by the author (2017).

Two of the parents chose the "Other" option and used the space to justify their choice. What was written by the interviewees is transcribed here in full.

"More or less, because some days there are things she can't do and sometimes she comes home complaining that I sit while the kids play **ball." (FATHER I).**

"He likes it a lot but we know there are things he can't do. For example, when he throws the ball, it doesn't go because his arm is **too weak. Then there are things he won't play with the boys." (FATHER II).**

It can be seen from the parents' reports that the physical activity offered by the school is sometimes exclusionary, as it leaves out students who, because of their disability, are unable to keep up with their peers. It wasn't possible, in this interview, to ascertain the extent to which this occurs during lessons. It will be possible to find out in the future in another, more detailed field study.

Parents were asked if their children enjoyed taking part in PE lessons. The result was unanimously "Yes".

The parents were emphatic in saying that "It's the class he likes the most", "He waits all week for PE class on Friday", "Wow, he likes it the most", "He likes it because he can play with his mates", "I think it's the time he has the most fun and interacts with his friends".

Given this unanimity, we tried to find out why parents believe their children enjoy taking part in PE lessons. Several answers were given and most of them covered the issue of "interaction" and "playing" with other classmates.

One of the parents reported:

> **"I think he likes it because he can't** keep up with the content in the classroom. And there (during PE) he must feel the same as the others. I think he feels normal, right?! Because nobody likes to be different. And the boys often call him to play ball, because he's **good, you know?" (FATHER, III).**

In order to find out whether parents are aware of what happens at school in terms of PE activities, we tried to understand whether they are able to find out how many classes are offered during the week.

The majority of the 13 parents who took part in the survey replied that the school offers two lessons a week. And according to the information provided by the school, the answer is correct.

However, it was possible to notice that some parents had doubts before giving an answer. They were embarrassed when answering and asked questions, showing uncertainty. This can be seen in the transcripts below:

> "I think it's just one [...] um [...] or is there more? [...] I don't think so, it's just one." (FATHER II).

> "I don't know if it's on Tuesday or Wednesday [...] I think it's on Tuesday [...] so that should be it, right?" (FATHER IV).

> "Wow girl, last year it was on Friday [...] now this year [...] well [...] I think it's just one [...] I just can't tell you what day it is." (FATHER V).

The graphic sign [...] was used to show pauses during speech and embarrassment when giving an answer. It can be seen that some parents know that classes are organised only once, but they couldn't say what day of the week they are held.

Parents were asked where and how these classes take place. Most of them replied that they are held "on the court" and that the teacher puts them to "play". Some of the interviewees described it as follows:

> "The teacher gives both theoretical and practical lessons, because some days she takes a photocopied text home." (FATHER I).

> "Well, I know that on some days the teacher takes them to the court and on other days the lesson is in the classroom, when she copies texts about the rules of the games and they copy them in their notebooks" (FATHER V).

> "Some days it's on the court when it's a game. Some days it's in the playground when it's a game. Some days she takes them to the little square (in front of the school). Every day she gives them something different." (FATHER VI).

The parents were able to say where the PE lessons took place, but when asked how they took place, they responded with the activities that the teachers offered. They did not clearly explain how these physical exercises are taught.

Parents were asked if their children had ever been excluded from PE lessons for any reason. The majority were emphatic in answering "No". There were reports from some parents who said that some days their children didn't take part in classes, but that there was no "exclusion". Here are some of the parents' comments:

> "Not exclusion, but some days he can't take part because of his medication.". (FATHER VII).
>
> "I can't say she's excluded, but some days she can't play with her classmates because she can't run. But that's not the teacher's fault, right?" (FATHER VIII).
>
> "There were a few days when he missed PE lessons because he wasn't doing his homework in class. Then the teacher wouldn't let him go to PE class. [...] I feel sorry for him, but if they don't do that he won't obey, he's too lazy to copy from the board." (FATHER IX). (FATHER IX).

It was possible to see that parents believe that when the PE teacher carries out an activity that demands more than their child can offer, it is "normal" for them to be left out. Other interviewees believe that it is also "normal" for PE lessons to be used as a form of "punishment" or "reward".

Nogueira (2002) considers the deprivation of recess and Physical Education to be "consensual aggression". "Aggression" because it prevents students from interacting with others and from learning, because according to the author, you also learn by "playing". "Consent" because parents, even though they know their children are being punished, believe it to be a normal attitude and end up accepting it and sometimes even asking teachers to punish them.

The quality of the PE teacher's teaching with students with disabilities was another question raised during the interview. The answer options were "Excellent", "Good", "Fair" and "Other", as shown in Graph 27.

It can be seen that 46 per cent of those interviewed consider the work of the PE teacher to be "Excellent", while 39 per cent consider it to be "Good". And none of the parents rated this teacher as "Fair".

One of the parents said: "You have to know everything to say it's excellent, right? But I have nothing to complain about the teacher."

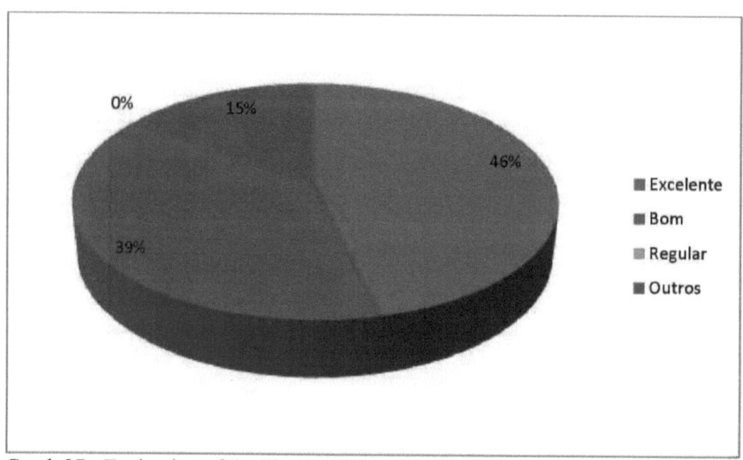

Graph 27 - Evaluation of the Physical Education teacher's work
Source: Organised by the author (2017).

Still on Graph 27, the parents who ticked "Other", totalling 15%, gave their reasons:

Once again, it can be seen that the parents didn't know exactly how the physical education classes are taught by the teacher. What they reported most is that the children like to "play" and that they like the teacher.

It is possible to infer that there is a lack of communication from the school regarding the actions, objectives and pedagogical practices used in Physical Education classes. Parents were unable to adequately describe the work of this professional.

Parents were also asked about the importance of PE lessons. Both were unanimous in saying that they are very important for their children.

Parents were asked "why" they think physical education classes are important for their children. There was a variety of answers, but the majority were: "Because he exercises", "Because it's good for his health", "Because he plays", "Because he interacts with his mates".

Comparing the answers given by the parents and the PCNs (1997), it can be seen that the vision that parents have in relation to Physical Education is only to look for exercises that promote the health and well-being of their child. They forget: valuing and respecting socio-cultural plurality; respecting rules and individual characteristics; caring for their own bodies; adopting hygiene and healthier habits for a better quality of life; using dialogue to mediate conflicts; historical and theoretical knowledge of sports, games and play; and exercising political, civil, social and personal rights and duties in everyday life and the other objectives that are described.

CHAPTER 5

5.1 FINAL CONSIDERATIONS

It can be seen that since the dawn of civilisation, human beings have always needed to act and practice bodily movements. Whether to attack or defend themselves, to hunt, dance or express their religiosity, or even their feelings.

In the Ancient Ages, in cities like Sparta in Greece, the cult of the body and fitness were already revered. The aim of Spartan education was to turn its citizens into strong, obedient and competent warriors. Even the great thinkers of the time, such as Plato, understood "gymnastics" as a union between body and thought.

It wasn't until 1423, in Italy, that the first "physical educator" appeared: Vittorino da Feltre understood that physical activity and its study should be aligned with the other subjects offered in schools. However, it wasn't until 432 years later that gymnastics became compulsory in the school curriculum.

It is currently a compulsory school subject throughout basic education, from kindergarten to high school. Scholars such as Bracht (1992) and Ferreira (2011) defend the importance of physical activity for the cognitive, affective, social and motor development of children and adolescents in schools. In addition to these benefits, Physical Education in schools helps to put an end to childhood obesity and stress - the evil of the century.

Activities such as games, sports, dances and fights are part of everyday life in mainstream schools. However, there is great concern about the clientele of PE teachers. This is because schools are regularly receiving students with disabilities, whether they be physical, cognitive or learning disabilities.

This public was already mentioned in the Law of Guidelines and Bases (1996) and in the National Curriculum Parameters (1997), but only now has the awareness of these students increased considerably, as their enrolment in public schools is no longer optional but compulsory.

Hence the emergence of what scholars call "Adapted Physical Education", which is the field of physical education (school or non-school) whose object of study is human motor skills for people with special educational needs. This area of physical education emerged in the 1950s, proposing diversified activities for people with some kind of disability who couldn't keep up with the strict programmes of the time, which sought brute force and the same result for all students.

In the activities carried out by PE teachers in schools, teaching methodologies are adapted to cater for the individual characteristics of each disabled student, respecting their differences, their limits and their unique abilities.

The first training course for physical educators was launched in 1929. Almost 90 years later, what was realised in the bibliographical research is that many scholars, such as Brito and Lima (2012), believe that neither schools nor Physical Education teachers are fully prepared to meet the requirements of the country's Inclusion laws. In their research, the authors heard from the teachers themselves that they don't feel prepared to deal with inclusion.

It is believed that the training of Physical Education professionals cannot be achieved in a purely practical-theoretical or intellectual capacity, but must encompass the scientific, technological, social and ethical transformations of modern society. It must start from a biological vision to one that combines the cognitive, affective and socio-cultural dimensions of the students, whether this training is a bachelor's degree or an undergraduate degree.

The field research for this study took place in the city of Caldas Novas-GO in the second half of 2016. There are currently 18 municipal schools, but one of them does not offer mainstream education, but only caters for people with disabilities. Therefore, 17 municipal schools took part in the research. In these schools, there are 20 Physical Education teachers working in the municipality who were the focus of the research.

A questionnaire was sent to the teachers and coordinators of the school where he works. In addition, an interview was conducted with the guardians of disabled students enrolled at the school, in order to understand how accessibility or inclusion of these students in Physical Education classes occurs.

It was possible to find out the profile of these professionals who work in Physical Education in municipal schools. The majority of these teachers are male, between 40 and 50 years old, cater for 1 to 5 year olds with disabilities, and carry out adapted activities for the students. As for the pupils, most of them have a medical certificate, take part in PE lessons, have a good relationship with their classmates, their behaviour varies from quiet to aggressive, they learn what they are taught and show concern for their health.

During the research with PE teachers, it was identified that some have non-specific training for working in schools, contrary to the law that requires a full degree in physical education.

We also realised that some teachers didn't have access to their student's medical report, so some didn't even identify how many disabled students they had in their classes. This failure is either due to a lack of training in the area of Special Education and/or Inclusion, or to a lack of communication between parents and the school, or even between the school and the teacher.

Teachers receive lectures and continuing education courses in the area of Special Education and Inclusion from the municipality, but it was identified that this training is joint with the other teachers, and there is no specific training for physical educators.

Another relevant item found in the research is the divergent behaviour of students with disabilities during PE lessons, classified by teachers as "aggressive" or "apathetic". This is usually due to the teacher's lack of information about the behavioural characteristics of the student's disability. It is understood that just knowing the name of the disability is not satisfactory; it is necessary to study how they react to certain stimuli.

A total of 17 coordinators answered the questionnaire, one from each municipal school. It was possible to see that: the majority are female, aged between 40 and 50, all are graduates and have postgraduate degrees in various areas, some of which are different from education, the majority rate the work of the PE teacher as excellent. According to them, the school is fully accessible, they have between 1 and 14 students with disabilities, totalling 68, both of whom take part in PE lessons.

The evaluation of the questionnaire answered by the 17 municipal coordinators showed that most parents are not concerned about the physical and motor development of their child with a disability. Some don't find out what or how Physical Education is taught, others don't take their children's reports with them and still others don't take their children to the specialists recommended by the school itself.

An invitation was sent to the parents of the 68 students with disabilities, via the school, so that they could turn up on a scheduled day and time to be interviewed. There were no results from some schools, only 13 parents (guardians) in total turned up for the survey.

The profile of the parents is described, for the most part, as: female, married, aged between 30 and 40, complete secondary education. Parents say that their children participate in and enjoy PE lessons because it promotes interaction between classmates and is an opportunity to play. They know the days of the PE lessons and consider the teacher to be excellent.

Parents were unable to clearly state how physical education classes are taught. It was possible to see that the parents' view of these classes is distorted from the reality that has permeated the PCNs since the 90s. It is understood that it is not "normal" for students to be left out of the activities proposed by the teacher, nor to be left without PE because they didn't behave well or didn't do a previous activity.

Drawing a parallel between the objectives raised at the beginning of this work, it can be concluded that there is accessibility for students with disabilities in Physical Education classes. These classes highlight the students' limitations and abilities and encourage them to strive for better performance. The pedagogical practices used by professionals in the field are diversified and adapted, promoting interaction with other students.

5.2 RECOMMENDATIONS

In light of the research carried out and the data compiled and analysed, it is possible to come up with some recommendations for improving accessibility for students with disabilities in municipal schools in the city of Caldas Novas, Goiás. These suggestions are made to the people who were directly involved in the research.

It is recommended that teachers seek further training in the field of education, focussing on Adapted Physical Education, which aims to promote physical activities for people with disabilities as well as for other students. It is understood that with this, the teacher will be better able to deal with the varieties of humour that arise during lessons. In addition, it is recommended that teachers seek access to the medical or clinical reports of their students with disabilities. Whether through parents or the school office, it is understood that the more we know about the student's history, the less chance there is of errors.

It is recommended that the coordinators, together with the municipality, seek out training courses or further training for their teachers. However, the focus should be on the specific disability of the school's clientele, and this training should be specifically for Physical Education teachers.

Communication should be an important tool for promoting accessibility for students with disabilities. It is therefore recommended that coordinators maintain a dialogue with teachers, informing them of the students' real situation, presenting the reports and seeking solutions to the problems encountered. When communicating with parents, the coordinator should inform and/or publicise more about the procedures for PE lessons and their purpose in the school.

Parents are advised to be more attentive to what happens at school. Monitoring your child's physical and cognitive development requires dedication and daily participation in their school life. It is understood that by knowing what is offered in PE classes and why, parents can help them and even the school to fulfil their role.

Another recommendation for parents is to seek a report from a specialist doctor in the area of their child's disability. What we noticed in the survey was the number of students without a medical report (who didn't take part in the survey), with medical reports without details or a description of the disability (some only presented a prescription from a general practitioner as proof of the disability), or with illegible handwriting. There are also parents who didn't present the medical report at the school office. It is understood that by doing this, the parent will facilitate the educators' work with the child.

BIBLIOGRAPHICAL REFERENCES

ALBUQUERQUE, Carlos. **Caldas Novas:** beyond the hot springs. Caldas Novas/GO: Kelps, 1996.

BRACHT, Valter. **Social learning and Physical Education.** Porto Alegre: Magister, 1992.

BRITO, Raull Felippe de Almeida; LIMA, João Franco. **Adapted Physical Education and Inclusion:** challenges faced by Physical Education teachers in working with students with disabilities. Revista UniJorge ISSN 2238-300X. 2012.

BRAZIL. **Law No. 4.024/61.** National Education Guidelines and Bases Law - LDBEN. Available at: <https://www.planalto.gov.br/ccivil_03/leis/L4024.htm>. Accessed on: 10 Dec. 2015.

. **Law No. 5.692/71.** National Education Guidelines and Bases Law - LDBEN. Available at: <http://www.planalto.gov.br/ccivil_03/leis/L5692.htm>. Accessed on: 05 Dec. 2015.

. **Law No. 6.251/75.** National Physical Education and Sports Policy Available at: <https://www.planalto.gov.br/ccivil_03/leis/1970-1979/L6251 .htm>. Accessed on: 12 Dec. 2015.

. **Law No. 9.394/96.** National Education Guidelines and Bases Law - LDBEN. Available at: <http://www.planalto.gov.br/ccivil_03/leis/L9394.htm>. Accessed on: 11 December 2015.

. **National Curriculum Parameters:** Physical Education. Department of Basic Education. - Brasília: MEC/SEF, 1997.

______ . **Resolution Cne/Cp 1** of 18 February 2002. Establishes National Curriculum Guidelines for Teacher Training. Available at: <http://portal.mec.gov.br/cne/arquivos/pdf/rcp01_02.pdf>. Accessed on 16 January 2016.

______ . **Resolution No. 7 of 31 March 2004.** Available at: <http://portal.mec.gov.br/cne/arquivos/pdf/ces0704edfisica.pdf>. Accessed on 10 March 2016.

______ . **CIVIL APPEAL N. 0013853-04.2011.4.01.3500/GO.** Federal Regional Court of the First Region. Available at: <http://cref14.org.br/dow/licenciatura_acordao.pdf>. Accessed on: 08 May 2016.

. **Law No. 12.764** of 27 December 2012. Regulation establishing the National Policy for the Protection of the Rights of People with Autism Spectrum Disorders. Available at: < http://www.planalto.gov.br/ccivil_03/_ato2011-2014/2012/lei/l12764.htm>. Accessed on: 12 July 2016.

. **Provisional Measure 746** of 22 September 2016. Establishes a policy to promote the implementation of full-time secondary schools. Available at: < http://www.planalto.gov.br/ccivil_03/_Ato2015-2018/2016/Mpv/mpv746.htm>. Accessed on 16 April 2016.

CARVALHO, Maria Isabel Gonçalves. **School/family, felt relationship and dreamed relationship:** a case study in a multicultural context. Dissertation (Master's Degree in Educational Sciences). Faculty of Psychology and Educational Sciences, University of Lisbon, 1998.

CASTELLANI FILHO, Lino. . **Physical Education in Brazil:** The Untold Story. 15. ed. Campinas - SP: Editora Papirus, 2008.

CAPINUSSÚ, José Maurício. **Physical activity in the Middle Ages:** bravery and loyalty above all else. Rio de Janeiro: UFRJ, 2005.

CIDADE, R. E.; FREITAS, P. S. **Educação Física e Inclusão:** Considerações para a Prática Pedagógica na Escola. Integração, v. 14 - Special Issue - Adapted Physical Education, p. 27-30, 2002.

CONFEF - Federal Council of Physical Education. 2002. **School Physical Education.** E.F. MAGAZINE N° 05 - DECEMBER 2002. Available at: <http://www.confef.org.br/extra/revistaef/show.asp?id=3457>. Accessed on: 10 June 2015.

FARIA JÚNIOR, Alfredo Gomes de; FARINATTI, Paulo de Tarso Veras (eds.). **Research and production of knowledge in Physical Education.** Rio de Janeiro: SBDEF, 1992.

FERREIRA. A. B. H. **Novo Dicionário Aurélio da Língua Portuguesa.** 3. ed. São Paulo: Positivo, 2004.

FERREIRA, Gabriele. **What are the benefits of physical education in high school.** 2011. Available at: <https://canaldoensino.com.br/blog/quais-os-beneficios-da-educacao-fisica-no-ensino-medio>. Accessed on: 14 Dec. 2016.

FREIRE, João B. **Full-body education:** theory and practice of physical education. 3. ed. Rio de Janeiro: Scipione, 1992.

GADOTTI, Moacir. **Citizen School.** 2. ed. São Paulo: Cortez, 1993.

GIL, A. C. **Como elaborar projetos de pesquisa.** 4. ed. São Paulo: Atlas, 2008.

GORGATTI, M. G.; COSTA, R. F. **Adapted Physical Activity.** Barueri - SP: Manole, 2005.

IBGE. **Brazilian Institute of Geography and Statistics.** Census 2015. Available at: <http://www.ibge.gov.br/censo/defau.php>. Accessed on: 19 September 2016.

LAKATOS, E. M.; MARCONI, M. A. **Fundamentos de metodologia científica.** 5. ed. São Paulo: Atlas, 2003.

MANTOAN, M. T. E. **School Inclusion:** What is it? Why? How to do it? How to do it? São Paulo: Editora Moderna, 2003.

MARINHO, Inezil P. **História da Educação Física e dos Desportos no Brasil.** Rio de Janeiro: Ebal, 1980.

MEC. **Government launches New High School, with Full-Time Schools and new curriculum proposal.** Available at: <http://portal.mec.gov.br/ultimas-noticias/211-218175739/39571-proposta-preve- flexibilizaçãoo-e-r-1-5-bilhao-em-investimentos-em-schools-de-tempo-integral>. Accessed on: 13 April 2017.

MIQUELIN, Eric Carvalho; FERNANDES, Mara Cléia et al. **Physical education and its benefits for primary school students.** 2014. Available at: <https://www.inesul.edu.br/revista/arquivos/arq- idvol_32_1421443852.pdf>. Accessed on: 16 Dec. 2016.

NOGUEIRA, Martha Guanaes. **Homework:** Consented Violence? São Paulo: Loyola, 2002.

OLIVEIRA, Vitor Marinho de. **What is Physical Education?** 11. ed. São Paulo: Brasiliense, 2006.

PORTAL EDUCAÇÃO. **Benefits of Physical Education.** 2014. Available at: <>. Accessed on: 10 December 2016.

PRODANOVI, C. C.; FREITAS, E. C. **Metodologia do Trabalho Científico:** métodos e técnicas da pesquisa e do trabalho acadêmico. 2. ed. Novo Hamburgo: Feevale, 2013.

RAMOS, Jayr Jordão. **Physical Exercise in History and Art:** from primitive man to the present day. São Paulo: IBRASA, 1982.

RODRIGUES, Ingrid Vieira. **The importance of practising Physical Education in Primary School.** 2013. Available at: <http://www.portaleducacao.com.br/educacao/artigos/47188/a-importancia-da- praticada-educacao-fisica-no-ensino-fundamental-i>. Accessed on: 13 Dec. 2016.

SILVA, Rita de Fátima; SEABRA JÚNIOR, Luiz; ARAÚJO, Paulo Ferreira. **Adapted Physical Education in Brazil:** from History to Educational Inclusion. São Paulo: Phorte, 2008.

VYGOTSKY, L. S. **Imagination and art in childhood: a** psychological essay. Madrid: Akal, 1982.

TAFFAREL, C. N. Z. **Creativity in physical education classes** (1985) IN: Parâmetros Curriculares Nacionais: Educação Física. Department of Elementary Education. - Brasília: MEC/SEF, 1997.

Printed by Books on Demand GmbH, Norderstedt / Germany